THE FEDERAL EMPLOYEES FAMILY FRIENDLY LEAVE ACT

HEARING

BEFORE THE

SUBCOMMITTEE ON
COMPENSATION AND EMPLOYEE BENEFITS

OF THE

COMMITTEE ON
POST OFFICE AND CIVIL SERVICE
HOUSE OF REPRESENTATIVES

ONE HUNDRED THIRD CONGRESS

SECOND SESSION

MAY 18, 1994

Serial No. 103–44

Printed for the use of the Committee on Post Office and Civil Service

U.S. GOVERNMENT PRINTING OFFICE

83–201 WASHINGTON : 1994

For sale by the U.S. Government Printing Office
Superintendent of Documents, Congressional Sales Office, Washington, DC 20402
ISBN 0-16-046198-7

COMMITTEE ON POST OFFICE AND CIVIL SERVICE

WILLIAM L. CLAY, Missouri, *Chairman*

PATRICIA SCHROEDER, Colorado	JOHN T. MYERS, Indiana
FRANK McCLOSKEY, Indiana	BENJAMIN A. GILMAN, New York
GARY L. ACKERMAN, New York	DON YOUNG, Alaska
THOMAS C. SAWYER, Ohio	DAN BURTON, Indiana
PAUL E. KANJORSKI, Pennsylvania	CONSTANCE A. MORELLA, Maryland
ELEANOR HOLMES NORTON, District of Columbia	THOMAS J. RIDGE, Pennsylvania
BARBARA-ROSE COLLINS, Michigan	THOMAS E. PETRI, Wisconsin
LESLIE L. BYRNE, Virginia	SHERWOOD L. BOEHLERT, New York
MELVIN L. WATT, North Carolina	(Vacancy)
ALBERT RUSSELL WYNN, Maryland	
GREG LAUGHLIN, Texas	
SANFORD D. BISHOP, JR., Georgia	
SHERROD BROWN, Ohio	
ALCEE L. HASTINGS, Florida	

GAIL E. WEISS, *Staff Director*
ROBERT E. LOCKHART, *General Counsel*
DORIS MOORE-GLENN, *Deputy Staff Director*
JOSEPH A. FISHER, *Minority Staff Director*

SUBCOMMITTEE ON COMPENSATION AND EMPLOYEE BENEFITS

ELEANOR HOLMES NORTON, District of Columbia, *Chair*

GARY L. ACKERMAN, New York	CONSTANCE A. MORELLA, Maryland
LESLIE L. BYRNE, Virginia	DON YOUNG, Alaska

CEDRIC HENDRICKS, *Subcommittee Staff Director*

CONTENTS

MAY 18, 1994

	Page
Hearing held in Washington, DC, May 18, 1994	1
Statement of:	
Bowling, Timothy P., Associate Director, Federal Human Resource Management Issues, General Government Division, General Accounting Office, accompanied by Robert Shelton	11
Green, Lorraine, Deputy Director, Office of Personnel Management, accompanied by Barbara Fisk, Associate Director for Personnel Systems and Oversight	2
Harnage, Robert, national secretary-treasurer, American Federation of Government Employees; Sheila Velazco, president, National Federation of Federal Employees; Susan Shaw, legislative liaison, National Treasury Employees Union; and Carolyn Kroon, president, Federally Employed Women	20
Prepared statements, letters, supplemental materials, et cetera:	
Bowling, Timothy P., Associate Director, Federal Human Resource Management Issues, General Government Division, General Accounting Office, prepared statement of	14
Chatel, Mary, president, National Council Social Security Management Associations, Inc., prepared statement of	36
Federal Managers Association, prepared statement of	35
Green, Lorraine, Deputy Director, Office of Personnel Management:	
Prepared statement of	4
Response to written questions submitted by Hon. Eleanor Holmes Norton	5
Harnage, Robert, national secretary-treasurer, American Federation of Government Employees, prepared statement of	21
Kroon, Carolyn, president, Federally Employed Women, prepared statement of	28
Morella, Hon. Constance A., a Representative in Congress from the State of Maryland, prepared statement of	31
Tobias, Robert M., president, National Treasury Employees Union, prepared statement of	25
Velazco, Sheila, president, National Federation of Federal Employees, prepared statement of	23

THE FEDERAL EMPLOYEES FAMILY FRIENDLY LEAVE ACT

WEDNESDAY, MAY 18, 1994

HOUSE OF REPRESENTATIVES,
COMMITTEE ON POST OFFICE AND CIVIL SERVICE,
SUBCOMMITTEE ON COMPENSATION AND EMPLOYEE BENEFITS,
Washington, DC.

The subcommittee met, pursuant to call, at 2:28 p.m., in room 311, Cannon House Office Building, Hon. Eleanor Holmes Norton (chair of the subcommittee) presiding.

Members present: Representatives Norton and Morella.

Ms. NORTON. The hearing is convened.

Today we hold a hearing on H.R. 4361, the Federal Employees Family Friendly Leave Act, which I introduced on May 5, 1994. The first part of the bill provides that in addition to any other allowable purpose, sick leave may be used by an employee to give care or otherwise attend to a family member of the employee having an illness, injury, or other condition which, if an employee had the condition, would justify the use of sick leave by that employee.

Currently, Federal employees are permitted only to use their sick leave for their own illnesses, pregnancies, or if someone in their immediate family has a contagious disease.

The second part of the bill provides that Federal employees may donate and receive annual leave for any reason from family members who also work for the Federal Government. However, in order to be eligible to receive a transfer of an annual leave, the leave transfer must not cause the total amount of annual leave available to the employee to exceed 240 hours. In addition, employees would not be able to cash out transferred leave upon leaving Government service.

Both parts of the bill would be authorized for a 3-year period, and, not later than 6 months before the authority sunsets, the Office of Management and Budget would submit a report to Congress evaluating the use of this authority and making recommendations as to whether or not it should be continued.

Analysis of existing Federal Government leave policy shows the need and desire for this legislation. The report of the National Performance Review states that—and I am quoting: "Family friendly policies serve the needs of a diverse work force struggling to manage child care, elder care, family emergencies, and other personal responsibilities while at the same time remaining committed to professional development and advancement." The NPR went on to recommend that employees be permitted to use sick leave to care for dependents in order to advance these goals.

In addition, the Bureau of Labor Statistics found that in the private sector 36 percent of employees are already granted the right by their employers to use sick leave to care for a sick child. OPM found that 46 State governments whose sick leave approval policies are generally comparable to those of the Federal Government allow use of sick leave for family illnesses. The General Accounting Office conducted a study that found that several private sector employers allowed employees to use all or a portion of their paid sick leave to care for immediate family members who were ill. Today GAO will expand on these findings. GAO will also share the results of its report that examines how Federal employees feel about the Federal Government as a place to work.

On May 11, 1994, OPM published an interim regulation to, among other things, permit Federal employees to use up to 5 days of their accrued sick leave to care for a sick child, spouse, or parent. This OPM proposal is not as far-reaching as my bill. During the hearing today, I want to explore the differences between my bill and OPM's regulations.

Today, in addition to OPM, we will hear also from the GAO and organizations representing Federal employees as well as Federal employed women. I welcome all of today's witnesses and very much look forward to hearing your testimony.

May I ask the first witness to come forward, the Honorable Lorraine Green, Deputy Director, Office of Personnel Management.

STATEMENT OF HON. LORRAINE GREEN, DEPUTY DIRECTOR, OFFICE OF PERSONNEL MANAGEMENT, ACCOMPANIED BY BARBARA FISS, ASSOCIATE DIRECTOR FOR PERSONNEL SYSTEMS AND OVERSIGHT

Ms. GREEN. Good afternoon, Madam Chair.

For the record, I am Lorraine Green, the Deputy Director of the Office of Personnel Management, and joining me at the table today is Barbara Fiss, the Associate Director for Personnel Systems and Oversight. I am pleased to be here today to discuss a topic that is a priority of this administration, family friendly leave policies.

The bill you have introduced, Madam Chair, has two components. It would make a Federal employee's sick leave available without limitation for use in caring for a family member of the employee who is sick or injured. The second part of your bill would amend the Federal Employees Voluntary Leave Transfer Program to permit an employee to transfer annual leave to a family member of the employee for reasons other than a medical emergency.

Let me begin by addressing the first part of your bill. I am pleased to inform you that OPM has recently published proposed sick leave regulations allowing Federal employees to use up to 5 days of sick leave each year to provide a family member with care needed because of illness, injury, pregnancy, or childbirth. The regulations also would permit use of sick leave, subject to the 5-day limit, to make arrangements required by the death of a family member or to attend the funeral of a family member. We believe this change will serve both employees and the Government as an employer.

The Government needs to adopt policies that will enable it to recruit and retain high quality employees who, when they are on the job, will be focused on serving their customers and not distracted by worries about the safety and health of their family members. Moreover, the Government, as a model employer, needs to set an example for other employers who may fear that family friendly policies will impede their ability to provide top quality customer service. Family friendly policies produce employees who are more loyal to their employer and more committed to carrying out the mission of their agency efficiently and effectively.

Our proposed regulations do differ from your bill in placing a 5-day limit on the amount of sick leave that could be used by an employee each year for caring for a family member. We believe this limit will ensure that employees will continue to have sufficient sick leave to meet their own needs in the event of illness.

Federal employees earn 13 days of sick leave each year. The average employee uses 8 days of sick leave a year, leaving 5 days unused. Consequently, we believe a 5-day limit on the use of sick leave to care for family members will be adequate and appropriate in the vast majority of cases.

Our proposed regulations on sick leave would also change the current rule which allows former Federal employees who return to service to have their unused sick leave recredited only if their break in Federal employment lasted no more than 3 years. Our proposed regulations would eliminate the 3-year limit so that sick leave would be recredited to the employee regardless of the duration of the break in Federal service. We believe employees would be more likely to use sick leave responsibly if they know that they can accrue and maintain a substantial sick leave balance and count on having it remain to their credit even if their Federal careers are interrupted, such as a parent who chooses to interrupt his or her career for a few years to care for a young child.

The second part of your bill, Madam Chair, concerns the voluntary leave transfer program. Currently the law governing our leave transfer program allows employees to share annual leave only in the event of a medical emergency. Your bill would allow transfers of annual leave for any purpose between employees who are related. While this measure would be welcomed by some employees, it would expand the leave-sharing program substantially beyond its original purpose, which was to allow employees to help their coworkers maintain income during a medical emergency. We are concerned that this particular expansion may be perceived as unfair to the vast majority of employees who do not have relatives employed by the Federal Government.

To conclude my testimony, I would say that the objectives of this bill and of the administration's new sick leave regulations are remarkably similar. We all agree that family friendly leave policies are essential to creating a highly qualified and motivated work force. However, we believe it is preferable to approach this objective through the regulatory process first—to invite and evaluate comments from all interested parties which we can take into account in developing final regulations, and then we can always further revise the regulations if need be, based on experience.

Again, thank you for inviting me here today, and I would be happy to answer any questions you may have.

[The prepared statement of Ms. Green follows:]

Prepared Statement of Lorraine Green, Deputy Director, Office of Personnel Management

Madam Chair and members of the subcommittee, I am pleased to be here today to discuss a topic that is a priority of this administration—family-friendly leave policies.

The bill you have introduced, Madam Chair, has two components. It would make a Federal employee's sick leave available, without limitation, for use in caring for a family member of the employee who is sick or injured. The second part of your bill would amend the Federal Employees' Voluntary Leave Transfer Program to permit an employee to transfer annual leave to a family member of the employee for reasons other than a medical emergency.

Let me begin by addressing the first part of your bill. I am pleased to inform you that OPM has just published proposed sick leave regulations implementing recommendations of the National Performance Review. These regualtions would allow Federal employees to use up to 5 days of sick leave each year to provide a family membee with care needed because of illness, injury, pregnarcy, or childbirth. The regulations also would permit use of sick leave—subject to the 5-day limit—to make arrangements required by the death of a family member or to attend the funeral of a family member.

We at OPM believe this change will serve both employees and the Government as an employer. The Government needs to adopt policies that will enable it to recruit and retain high-quality employees who, when they are on the job, will be forcused on serving their customers and not distracted by worries about the safety and health of their family members. Moreover, the Government, as a model employer, needs to set an example for other employers who may fear that family-friendly policies will impede their ability to provide top quality customer service. Famil-friendly polices produce employees who are more loyal to their employer and more committed to carrying out the mission of their agency efficiently and effectively.

Our proposed regulations do differ from your bill in placing a 5-day limit on the amount of sick leave that could be used by an employee each year for caring for a family member. We beleive this limit makes sense as a means of ensuring that employees will continue to have sufficient sick leave to meet their own needs in the event of illness.

Federal employees earn 13 days of sick leave each year. The average employee uses 8 day of sick leave a year, leaving 5 days unused. Consequenbtly, we believe a 5-day limit on the use of sick leave to care for family member will be adequate and appropriate in the vast majority of cases.

Our proposed regulations on sick leave would also change the current rule which allows former Federal employees who return to Federal service to have their unused sick leave recredited only if their break in federal employment lasted no more than 3 years. Our proposed regulations would eliminate the 3-year limit, so that sick leave would be recredited to the employee regardless of the duration of the break in Federal service. We believe employees will be more likely to use sick leave responsibly if they know that they can accrue and maintain a substantial sick leave balance and count on having it remain to their credit, even if their Federal careers are interrupted—such as a parent who chooses to interrupt his or her career for a few years to care for a young child.

The second part of your bill, Madam Chair, concerns the Voluntary Leave Transfer Progam. Curently, the law governing our Leave Transfer Program allows employees to share annual leave only in the event of a medical emergency. Your bill would allow transfers of annual leave for any purpose between employees who are related. While this measure would be welcomed by some employees, it would expand the Leave Sharing Program substantially beyond its original purpose, which was to allow employees to help their coworkers maintain income during a medical emergency. We are concerned that this particular expansion may be perceived as unfair to the vast majority of employees who do not have relatives employed by the Federal Government.

To conclude my testimony, I would say that the objectives of this bill and of the administration's new sick leave regulations are remarkably similar. Family-friendly leave policies are essential to creating a highly qualified and motivated work force. However, we believe it is preferable to approach this objective through the regulatory process first—to invite and evaluate comments from all interested parties, which we can take into account in developing final regualtions—and then we can always further revise the regulations, if need be, based on experience.

RESPONSE TO WRITTEN QUESTIONS SUBMITTED BY HON. ELEANOR HOLMES NORTON TO LORRAINE GREEN

Question. Please provide information on the ability of agencies to cover positions in the face of increased absences resulting from greater use of sick and annual leave.

Answer. The ability of agencies to cover absences will probably vary significantly due to a variety of circumstances, including the kind of work performed (e.g., operational or staff work; health, safety, and other vital services), demands for contact with the public (e.g., serving the public directly versus providing support), amount of supervision needed to perform the work, adequacy of current staffing, agency and supervisory styles, etc.

Several agencies have experienced problems with the management of sick leave. OPM does not maintain Governmentwide data on individual agency leave management problems. Generally, however, most agencies handle sick leave abuse on an individual basis through counseling, monitoring, training, and when necessary, disciplining employees.

Any additional opportunities to use sick leave will make the management of sick leave more difficult for individual agencies and supervisors, especially during a period when a general Governmentwide downsizing effort will place even greater emphasis on maximizing individual and organizational productivity.

Question. What does OPM estimate the cost to the Federal government would be of the use of sick leave under H.R. 4361? Under OPM's proposed regulations?

Answer. The Government does not normally incur additional payroll costs when an employee uses sick leave. An employee's annual salary is paid for work performed and during periods of paid leave or excused absence. In some circumstances, an agency may have to order and approve overtime work by other employees to keep an operation running around the clock (e.g., police, fire protection, inspections, maintenance, security) or to complete work when tight deadlines are involved.

There is a loss in productivity to the Government when employees use sick leave, but we have no reliable measure of that loss. However, if one equates the use of 1 hour of sick leave to a loss in productivity of 1 hour of basic pay, the productivity loss could be expressed on a cost-per-hour basis. The current average hourly rate of basic pay for white-collar employees is $18.39 per hour. If that rate of pay is multiplied by the approximately 2.1 million civilian non-postal employees, the cost of 1 hour of sick leave for the entire employee population would be more than $38 million. The cost-per-day for 8 hours of sick leave for this same population would be more than $308 million.

Assessing costs in this manner, the OPM proposed rule change would result in a maximum loss in productivity of $1.544 billion, assuming that every employee in the CPDF population used the additional 5 days. Since there is no limit on the amount of additional sick leave that an employee may use for family care under H.R. 4361, it is impossible to estimate potential costs.

In the NFC data referenced above, the average employee had a sick leave balance of 468 hours (58.5 days). If all employees in the CPDF population used all their accrued sick leave, the total maximum cost exposure for H.R. 4361 for sick leave use would be $18.073 billion—more than 11 times the maximum potential cost of OPM's proposal.

Ms. NORTON. Thank you very much, Ms. Green.

Now your testimony: what I would like to explore first is the definition of a family member. How has the OPM interpreted the definition used in my bill in the context of the present leave sharing law?

Ms. GREEN. They are similar—they are the same in your bill and the leave sharing.

Ms. NORTON. I am now referring to the present leave sharing law. Could you provide some examples of who has been considered a family member under those regulations?

Ms. GREEN. The parents, spouse, child, in-laws of the spouse, the sisters, brothers, and any other individuals who are related by blood or affinity whose relationship is the equivalent of a family relationship. So it is a very broad definition.

Ms. NORTON. Why, in your regulations, is the definition so narrow, limited to parents, spouse, and child?

Ms. GREEN. The initiatives that we were moving forth with on these regulations were discussed in the National Performance Review, and we were trying to be consistent with the Family and Medical Leave Act definition, which was the spouse, child, and parent.

Ms. NORTON. So does that mean you are going to change—do you want to retrench from where you are?

Ms. GREEN. No. We are trying to be consistent with the Family and Medical Leave Act.

Ms. NORTON. I understand that. I am saying, but you have used a broader definition before. Does that mean we can expect you to retrench on the definitions that you have used before?

Ms. GREEN. No, not necessarily. What we are going to do is, during the 60-day comment period, while we have these regulations out and are receiving comments, we are going to consider the comments that we get and reexamine the definitions.

Ms. NORTON. I would appreciate that.

Ms. GREEN. Certainly.

Ms. NORTON. You know, one of the reasons why we are embarked on locality pay, one of the reasons why we are seeing young people—if you go into colleges today, such as the one in California from which my son is graduating, you are going to be able to count on the fingers of one hand who wants to come to the Federal Government. That didn't used to be the case. The private sector is perceived as a much more exciting place and as a fairer place.

As a Washingtonian, it grieves me to see the Federal Government falls behind in its benefit and pay packages and then expects somehow to be competitive with the private sector. So the notion of constantly retrenching, these corners that are cut on Federal employees at every opportunity, you all are going to pay for that, and you are not going to find this committee saying fine, follow the worst in the private sector. We are never going to become competitive again. We had a whole big commission that says you all are out of the competition. There are small ways to get back into the competition.

One of the ways in which the Federal Government remained competitive all the time was that its salaries were not competitive—because they became competitive only in recent decades—it was because its benefit package looked better. Now increasingly the benefit package of the private sector, and, God help us, the States look better on sick leave. Under a Democratic administration, I expect better frankly.

What is the basis for your concerns that employees will use all their sick leave for their family and not have enough sick leave for themselves? How many employees exhaust all their sick leave? What percentage of your employees exhaust their sick leave?

Ms. GREEN. We don't know the percentage of employees who exhaust sick leave. We have figures that show us that the average use of sick leave is 8 days a year.

The question you asked about the concerns that we have for employees using all of their sick leave requires a two-pronged answer. One, you have the fairly new employees, who have little accumulated sick leave, and if they have a family member who requests that they provide care to them and then they turn around and have a medical emergency of their own, they have exhausted all of their sick leave. The main purpose of our sick leave program is to enable employees to maintain their income during personal sickness or injury. But the employee who has had a very short time in the Federal Government doesn't have much sick leave.

Then, on the other hand, you have the employee who is long term and who has accumulated many hours of sick leave, and if they have a family member who becomes ill, we have another issue there because then that family member will require long-term care immediately, and tomorrow that employee who has all this sick leave can come into their supervisor and state that they have to be gone for months, and this is with no prior approval.

We think it is important to have reasonable limits on the amount of time an employee can be absent from work on unscheduled leave when they are personally not ill because agencies cannot afford to incur additional costs because of overtime and temporary hires to replace a person that is critical because of this unscheduled leave. The loss of expertise may be acute with some long-term employees who, in many cases serve in very critical positions, and they are the persons who are likely to have elderly dependents. We have put the agencies in a position where they are all downsizing and they cannot hire replacements, so we will put them at a disadvantage.

So trying to take into consideration both sets of employees, we feel it would be more reasonable to have the 5 days, and then if they need to be out on prolonged care, they can do as they are doing now and request annual leave, which will give managers the opportunity to approve that annual leave.

Ms. NORTON. Ms. Green, for the first part of your answer, I don't know whether the concern that people, especially new people who don't have accumulated leave, might run out of their leave altogether and others who have accumulated leave might need it because of a long-term illness—I don't know whether to call that paternalism or maternalism, but it obviously is something that assumes that people cannot, when educated, plan their own lives for themselves. Of course, 46 State governments have what appears to be greater confidence in people's decisions to manage their own lives.

I do agree that it is incumbent upon the agency to make perfectly clear what the risks are but wonder whether you should be in it once you have made that clear. I mean who are you, the Federal Government, to say we are really doing this for your own good?

Isn't your role one of education, one of making sure that there is a thorough understanding of the risks and allowing people to manage their own lives in a country that does not provide a lot of child care or the benefits for people to take care of emergencies that arise?

I mean who is in the best position to make that decision, you or the person involved?

Ms. GREEN. The sick leave program as it is established now, Madam Chair, is to care for the employees because we don't have a short-term disability program in the Government.

Regarding who should make the determination, there has to be a balance between the needs of the employee and the needs of the employer.

The five days, as I stated in my opening statement, was just a matter of adding and subtracting. It could probably be any number just as long as the employees, as you say, realize what the risk is and the benefits of having accumulated sick leave for their own personal leave.

I am not familiar with, and I will have staff look at, this study about the 46 State governments, but there are some that certainly would have personal leave, that would look at the entire leave package and have personal leave rather than just annual or sick, and people could decide for themselves how they would use a chunk of leave that they would be given. So there are other alternatives, yes.

Ms. NORTON. Ms. Green, you would be more persuasive on the question of limits if you provided this committee, as I would ask you to do, with the relative use of sick leave by Federal employees. It looks like you at least have a rational basis for your five days. But if people don't exhaust their sick leave, if we are only talking about an average, which means that there are many, many people who don't use up most of their sick leave, the context in which the committee operates is one in which we are the only industrialized country that does not provide liberal leave benefits to care for sick children; we have no child care system in this country. I can't imagine what happens to somebody when they call a snow day. This is the context in which we operate. And, again, if the leave is available and can be carried over anyway, it is hard for me to see how you are in this.

Instead of carrying it over, people want to use leave in the ways that the bill indicates. Your notion that you are not going to be able to cover for these employees is something that the committee would like very much to receive information about because if, in fact, we thought—already I think that there is evidence beginning to accumulate that the 252,000 is going to be a day we live to rue because essentially the Congress has accepted OPM and the administration's notion of 252,000 drawn out of the air, and I am not convinced, especially based on the post office experience, that we are not going to have a ton of confusion, overwork, service confusion, and people just hopping out of the Federal Government.

Now this matter of covering for people is raised. I am going to ask you to within 30 days submit to this committee the detailed experience within the last several years of Federal employees' use of sick and annual leave.

Ms. GREEN. OK.

Ms. NORTON. That would help us, because we certainly don't want to create any more problems than may well be created by the shortages that may develop over the loss of employees in any case.

Ms. GREEN. Certainly.

[The information referred to follows:]

Please provide information on the relative use of sick leave by Federal employees. Please include (a) the percent of employees that exhaust their sick leave; (b) the average number of days of sick leave currently held by Federal employees; and (c) a comparison of the information between CSRS and FERS employees.

OPM RESPONSE

OPM maintains a central personnel data file (CPDF) with personnel data from most Executive Branch agencies, but OPM does not maintain a central leave file.

Separate agency payroll systems maintain leave data. Generally, agency personnel and payroll systems are not merged. However, as a result of a special study, OPM did receive leave data from the Department of Agriculture's National Finance Center (NFC) covering agencies serviced by the NFC for leave year 1991. These data are not a statistically valid sample of Federal Government employees. Nonetheless, we believe the data are useful to demonstrate current patterns and trends.

(a) Of the 329,433 employees in the NFC data base, 16,736 employees (5.08 percent) had either a zero or negative sick leave balance (due to advanced leave).

(b) The average number of days of sick leave credited to employees in the NFC data base as of the end of leave year 1991 was 58.5 days (468 hours). The average sick leave balance for men was 90.0 days (720 hours), and the average sick leave balance for women was 28.0 days (224 hours).

(c) There were 157,254 Civil Service Retirement System (CSRS) employees with an average sick leave balance of 101.5 days (812 hours) and 141,266 Federal Employees Retirement System (FERS) employees with an average sick leave balance of 20 days (160 hours). (The average years of Federal service of FERS employees is much less than that of CSRS employees.)

Ms. NORTON. I am concerned about the part of your testimony that said that this kind of leave may be perceived as unfair to employees who do not have relatives employed by the Federal Government. Oh, my. Oh, my. All I can say is shame. Those were the kinds of arguments that we heard against the Family Medical and Leave Act. Those are the kinds of arguments that we have heard against people who do not want progressive policies.

Of course there will be people who don't have relatives employed by the Federal Government, but are you serious that a fellow worker would resent the fact that a mother could get sick leave to take care of a sick child and that that is a good reason for denying that mother the right to use her sick leave to take care of a sick child? You really want the record to show that?

Ms. GREEN. Madam Chair, I was referring to the provision in your bill that would allow sharing of annual leave among Federally employed family members for any purpose.

Ms. NORTON. I am sorry. I beg your pardon. She says that is only annual leave.

Ms. GREEN. Yes. Historically, the Government has provided these same benefits to all employees based on length of service. With annual leave, you earn that based on your tenure, based on your seniority, and you have employees who have worked a long time in the Government to earn eight hours of annual leave, and they may be sitting next to someone who just came into the Government, but because they are related to a family member, they now have the ability to have additional days transferred to them where this longtime employee does not. So it is a seniority issue, too.

Ms. NORTON. I see. That is very different from sick leave. I am sorry. That is a mistake I made.

The annual leave notion is, as used by private employers, increasingly, a way to make up for not having other kinds of leave policies. I mentioned earlier the declaration of these snow days; we have had lots of them of late, for example. You say in your testimony that this has to do with how people ought to equitably divide family responsibilities, and I suppose a case can be made from that point of view again, by the kind of employer that would want to make that case. I am just being very well educated by where the Federal Government now comes down on these issues, and that the notion that the Federal Government used its leave policies, its benefit policies, to attract the best and the brightest apparently is not the policy of the OPM or the Federal Government any more.

Ms. GREEN. No, I think it is, Madam Chair, along with the other programs that we have in effect. These are just the basic provisions of our leave programs and the current regulations that we are operating under. So we may want to reexamine the entire leave program to ensure that, by making a particular specific change, we are not creating new inequities.

Ms. NORTON. Could I ask you then, I mean the notion that some may perceive inequity because a spouse happens to be living is not an argument that is lost on me. I think there is some validity to that argument. Could I ask you within 30 days to provide a suggestion to this committee how that equity question in particular might be evened out, what options would be available, because I do believe, at least on the face of it, that two employees similarly situated might indeed come out differently in that way. Is there a way or are there options for attending to that problem?

Ms. GREEN. Certainly.

[The information referred to follows:]

Please provide suggestions on how to better address the fairness issue relative to the transfer of annual leave between family members.

OPM RESPONSE

Permitting the transfer of annual leave between family members outside the parameters of the existing voluntary leave sharing program for medical emergencies would benefit only those Federal employees who have family members who are also Federal employees. We believe this benefit is unfair because it is unavailable to most employees. Given the inherent inequity of this proposal, OPM is unable to offer any suggestion that would make the proposal fair.

The proposal also uncouples the relationship between length of service and the amount of annual leave an employee accrues. This can only cause resentment throughout the workforce and additional and unpredictable work planning problems for management.

Female employees are generally more directly affected by the need to balance work and family responsibilities, and this can seriously affect the working lives of women. Transfer of annual leave between family members may very well lead to more inequitable distribution of family care responsibilities. To the extent that leave were donated to a female family member, that individual's career could be adversely affected as she spent a greater amount of time off the job caring for other family members.

Other concerns include:

Allowing the transfer of annual leave between family members may increase costs. For example, employees may seek to protect their "use or lose leave" by temporarily transferring it to a family member. The family member could then transfer the use or lose leave back in the next leave year, thus avoiding forfeiture.

Permitting lower graded employees to donate leave to higher graded family members would increase the cost of that leave to the Government if used in lump-sum leave payments.

SES employees have no limit on the carryover of annual leave from one year to the next. They could give a disproportionate amount of leave to another family member.

Transferring leave for any purpose dilutes the original, well-received purpose (family or personal medical emergency) of the leave sharing program.

Ms. NORTON. Thank you very much. I appreciate your testimony. It has been very useful.

Ms. GREEN. Thank you.

Ms. NORTON. Could I say while you are here, I mentioned, Ms. Green, the possibility that your concern about covering for employees during the downsizing, I believe that is a very valid concern, not only about this particular suggestion but generally, and I wonder if OPM is using any methodology to keep track of how this downsizing is affecting the work performance and productivity of agencies, because there is no question in my mind that this subcommittee is going to be having hearings at some point in the not too distant future on this and we would be asking for information.

Ms. GREEN. Certainly. I know we are in the process of data gathering, so we will make sure that we have that information when we come to testify before you.

Ms. NORTON. Thank you. I would hate the notion that we didn't do our homework ahead of time. And this is not you. The administration decided for deficit reduction purposes that it wanted a reduction of 252,000 employees, and it did so in a very responsible way fiscally by doing it with buy-outs, and we endorsed that, but we had no way and we still have no way to tell what the effect on the Federal service would be or on retention of Federal employees or recruitment of Federal employees.

OPM would do well to find some way to keep track of this, because the subcommittee does not want to hear when it has its first hearing on this that you do not know, and we would like very much for you to, from the very beginning, require agencies to, in fact, begin to know.

No private employer would ever have done the downsizing we did without doing a functional survey to see where it would leave its customers and clients. We did not do that, and we need to make sure that when we get at the end of the five years we do not have a torrent of criticism because of the way in which we went about the downsizing.

Ms. GREEN. Certainly. That is understood.

Ms. NORTON. Thank you very much for your very helpful testimony, Ms. Green.

Ms. GREEN. Thank you.

Ms. NORTON. May I now call Timothy P. Bowling, Associate Director, Federal Human Resource Management Issues, General Government Division of the GAO.

STATEMENT OF TIMOTHY P. BOWLING, ASSOCIATE DIRECTOR, FEDERAL HUMAN RESOURCE MANAGEMENT ISSUES, GENERAL GOVERNMENT DIVISION, GENERAL ACCOUNTING OFFICE, ACCOMPANIED BY ROBERT SHELTON

Mr. BOWLING. Thank you, Madam Chair.

I would like to introduce my colleague, Mr. Robert Shelton, who is accompanying me today.

With your permission, I would like to present a somewhat shortened version of my statement and provide the full text for the record.

I am pleased to appear here today to provide GAO's views on H.R. 4361, the Federal Employees Family Friendly Leave Act. The bill calls for a 3-year experiment involving two changes to the leave program for Federal employees. One change would allow family members who are Federal employees to share annual leave. The other would allow Federal employees to use their sick leave to attend to a family member's medical needs. In our opinion, experimentation with both of these changes is appropriate as they will help make the Government a more family friendly employer.

Our work has shown that the Federal Government is behind leading non-Federal employers in helping employees balance their working lives with their personal and family needs. Significant demographic changes in the country's work force, such as the large increase in the number of working women and two-earner households, have prompted many employers to redesign their human resource policies and programs. These employers find that family friendly programs can be beneficial to the company as well as to the employee because of the savings resulting from productivity gains and the enhanced recruitment and retention of quality workers.

The Federal Employees Leave Sharing Act of 1988 permits Federal employees to donate annual leave to other employees who are facing unpaid absences caused by personal or family medical emergencies. Under this program, family members, like other employees, can donate annual leave to each other only in cases where, No. 1, the donated leave is needed to meet a medical emergency and, No. 2, the leave recipient has exhausted all of his or her available leave.

H.R. 4361 would change this program to allow family members to share annual leave without either of these conditions being present. In effect, this change would make annual leave a resource to be shared by family members as they see fit.

We believe the proposed change is worth trying. It could be a very great benefit by permitting a family member with little or no annual leave to take time off from work by using leave from another family member with a higher leave balance. Allowing the spouse to share leave in such cases could be beneficial to the family, and it would not change the combined amount of leave the spouses could use during the year.

The results of a Federal employees survey we published in 1992 showed considerable interest in the idea of allowing family members to share annual leave. The survey revealed that about 30 percent of all respondents had spouses and/or parents, siblings, and children who also worked for the Federal Government. Fifty-two percent of these respondents said it was somewhat to very likely that they would share annual leave with their spouses or other family members in the following year if the law allowed it; 25 percent said that such an option would make them more likely to stay in Federal employment.

While it is not possible to predict the amount of annual leave family members would share, the proposed change should result in little, if any, additional payroll costs. The bill contains a number of controls to prevent employees from accumulating donated leave that they don't really plan to use and then cashing it in upon separation.

The only circumstance in which we could envision extra salary outlays being incurred would be cases where the leave recipients would be on leave without pay if leave donations were not made. To the extent that the program results in paid leave being substituted for unpaid leave, added salary, outlays would result. On the other hand, to the extent that employees who make leave donations receive smaller lump sum payments when they separate, savings would result.

Moreover, based on other employers' experiences, productivity gains and other advantages that might be realized from making the Government a more family friendly employer can more than offset any potential cost increases that the program might cause.

Until an Annual Leave Sharing Program is actually tried in the Government, its associated costs or savings cannot be reliably predicted. As a result, we believe the cost issue should be closely examined during the 3-year test of the proposed program.

In general, Federal employees are allowed to use sick leave only when they are ill or for medical and dental appointments. Sick leave may not be used when a family member is ill unless the family member has a contagious disease. H.R. 4361 would eliminate this restriction and allow employees to use sick leave when family members have conditions that would justify sick leave if they were employees. We believe experimentation with this change is appropriate in the interest of helping Federal employees cope with their work and family responsibilities.

Our work has shown that the practice of giving employees paid time off to care for ill family members is becoming quite common among leading non-Federal employers. In our report comparing Federal and non-Federal work family programs, we found that most of the non–Federal organizations we visited permitted employees to use all or a portion of their paid sick leave to care for family members who are ill.

A December 1993 report by the Bureau of National Affairs on the survey of 155 employers of varying sizes and industries confirmed our findings that many organizations allow employees to use sick leave for family members' illnesses. According to the report, 45 percent of the employers allowed salaried employees to use sick leave to care for a sick child, 32 percent allowed sick leave for care of an elderly relative, and 39 percent allowed sick leave for care for other family members.

Expanding the circumstances in which employees may use sick leave can increase their absences from work. Also, if employees substitute sick leave for annual leave they may now be taking to care for ill family members, their lump sum payments for unused annual leave could be larger when they separate from Federal service.

Like annual leave sharing, the proposed sick leave amendment could also increase Federal salary outlays in cases where employees would have otherwise used unpaid leave to care for ill family members.

However, any cost resulting from an increase in the use of paid sick leave could be eventually offset in part by reduced retirement system costs. Retiring employees covered by the civil service retirement system may count unused sick leave as service credits in the calculation of their retirement benefits. To the extent that greater amounts of sick leave are used to tend to family members' medical needs, pure service credits would be available in the retirement benefit calculations.

Within the overall context of Federal employment policies, the changes proposed by H.R. 4361 are perhaps relatively minor. For example, they do not change the amount of annual and sick leave employees accrue every year, yet by allowing employees more op-

83-201 O - 94 - 2

tions for using their leave, this legislation should go a long way toward helping many employees better manage their work, personal, and family responsibilities.

This concludes my prepared statement, Madam Chair. I would be pleased to answer any questions you might have.

[The prepared statement of Mr. Bowling follows:]

PREPARED STATEMENT OF TIMOTHY P. BOWLING, ASSOCIATE DIRECTOR, FEDERAL HUMAN RESOURCE MANAGEMENT ISSUES, GENERAL GOVERNMENT DIVISION, GENERAL ACCOUNTING OFFICE

The proposed legislation would establish a 3-year experiment allowing Federal employees to (1) share annual leave with family members who are also Federal employees and (2) use sick leave to attend to family members' medical needs. GAO believes experimentation with these changes is appropriate. By allowing employees more options for managing their leave, the bill would help make the Government a more "family friendly" employer. Programs that help employees balance their working lives with their personal and family needs can be cost effective and beneficial to both employers and employees.

The proposal for sharing annual leave among family members would not change the overall amount of annual leave available to Federal employees. However, by making annual leave a resource to be shared among family members, it would provide flexibility in how leave can be used. A GAO survey showed considerable interest in annual leave sharing among Federal employees who have family members working for the Government. Over half of these employees told GAO they were "somewhat" to "very" likely to participate in a family leave sharing program, and about 25 percent said the availability of such a program would make it more likely they would continue with their Federal careers.

The proposal to allow Federal employees to use sick leave to attend to family members' medical needs is consistent with GAO's findings that non-Federal employers often give their employees paid time off for this purpose. Like the annual leave proposal, this change would give employees greater options for using their leave without increasing the total amount of leave available to Federal employees.

Until the proposed changes are actually tried in the Government their associated costs, or savings, cannot be reliably predicted. However, GAO sees no reason to believe the changes will be costly. The cost issue should be examined carefully during the 3-year experiment.

Madam Chair and Members of the Subcommittee, I am pleased to appear here today to provide GAO's views on H.R. 4361, the "Federal Employees Family Friendly Leave Act."

The bill calls for a 3-year experiment involving two changes to the leave program for federal employees. One change would allow family members who are federal employees to share annual leave. The other would allow employees to use their sick leave to attend to family members' medical needs. In our opinion, experimentation with both of these changes is appropriate as they will help make the government a more "family friendly" employer.

Our work has shown that the federal government is behind leading nonfederal employers in helping employees balance their working lives with their personal and family needs.[1] Significant demographic changes in the country's workforce, such as the large increase in the number of working women and two-earner households, have prompted many employers to redesign their human resource policies and programs. These employers find that family friendly programs can be beneficial to the company as well as to the employee because of the savings resulting from productivity gains and the enhanced recruitment and retention of quality workers.

ANNUAL LEAVE SHARING AMONG FAMILY MEMBERS

The Federal Employees Leave Sharing Act of 1988, as amended, permits federal employees to donate annual leave to other employees who are facing unpaid absences caused by personal or family medical emergencies. As we reported in our May 1993 appearance before this subcommittee, the leave sharing program has

[1] See "The Changing Workforce: Comparison of Federal and Non-Federal Work/Family Programs and Approaches" (GAO/GGD–92–84, April 23, 1992).

proved to be quite successful and is widely supported by federal agencies and employees alike.

Under the current leave sharing program, family members, like other employees, can donate annual leave to each other only in cases where (1) the donated leave is needed to meet a medical emergency and (2) the leave recipient has exhausted all of his or her available leave. H.R. 4361 would change the program to allow family members to share annual leave without either of these conditions being present. In effect, this change would make annual leave a resource to be shared by family members as they see fit.

We believe the proposed change is worth trying in the government. It could be of great benefit by permitting a family member with little or no annual leave to take time off from work by using leave from another family member with a high leave balance. For example, we are aware of situations in which one spouse of a federal employee couple has used so much of his/her annual leave attending to their children's needs that family vacations are difficult to arrange. Or, one spouse may have worked longer for the government than the other spouse and accumulated more annual leave. In such cases, one spouse has ample leave, but the other doesn't. Allowing the spouses to share leave in such cases could be beneficial to the family, and it would not change the combined amount of leave the spouses could use during the year. Also, nothing in the bill changes the prerogative agencies now have to approve or deny employee requests to use annual leave.

The results of a federal employee survey we published in 1992[2] showed considerable interest in the idea of allowing family members to share annual leave. The survey revealed that about 30 percent of all respondents had spouses and/or parents, siblings, and children who also worked for the government. While this is a large number, it would undoubtedly be even larger if the survey had used the broader definition of family member included in the bill.[3] Fifty-two percent of these respondents said it was "somewhat" to "very" likely that they would share annual leave with their spouses or other family members in the following year if the law allowed it. Twenty-five percent said such an option would make them more likely to stay in federal employment.

While it is not possible to predict the amount of annual leave family members would share, the proposed change should result in little, if any, additional payroll costs. The bill contains a number of controls to prevent employees from accumulating donated leave they don't really plan to use and cashing it in upon separation. For example, it precludes leave donations if they would cause a recipient's leave balance to exceed 240 hours. This would mean that any member of the Senior Executive Service who has an annual leave balance of 240 hours or more would be ineligible to receive leave donations. The Senior Executive Service is not subject to the 240-hour leave carryover limitation imposed by law on other employees. Further, the bill provides that lump-sum payments for unused annual leave made to separating employees cannot include payments for any leave donations they received during their last year of employment. These provisions are in addition to the requirement already existing in the leave sharing program that employees generally cannot donate leave they otherwise could not use and would forfeit at the end of the leave year.

The only circumstances in which we could envision extra salary outlays being incurred would be cases where the leave recipients would be on leave-without-pay if leave donations were not made. To the extent that the program results in paid leave being substituted for unpaid leave, added salary outlays would result. On the other hand, to the extent that employees who make leave donations receive small lump-sum payments when they separate, savings would result. Moreover, based on other employers' experiences, productivity gains and other advantages that might be realized from making the government a more family friendly employer could more than offset any potential cost increases the program might cause.

Until an annual leave sharing program is actually tried in the government, its associated costs, or savings, cannot be reliably predicted. The cost issued should be closely examined during the 3-year test of the proposed program.

---

[2] *Federal Employment: How Federal Employees View the Government as a Place to Work* (GAO/GGD–92–91, June 18, 1992)

[3] The bill includes as family members the employee's spouse and the spouse's parents, children (including adopted children and children of a spouse), parents, brothers and sisters (and their spouses), and any individual related by blood or affinity whose close association with the employee is the equivalent of a family relationship.

USING SICK LEAVE TO CARE FOR ILL FAMILY MEMBERS

In general, federal employees are allowed to use sick leave only when they are ill or for medical and dental appointments. Sick leave may not be used when a family member is ill unless the family member has a contagious disease. H.R. 4361 would eliminate this restriction and allow employees to use sick leave when family members have conditions that would justify sick leave if they were employees. We believe experimentation with this change is appropriate in the interest of helping federal employees cope with their work and family responsibilities.

Our work has shown that the practice of giving employees paid time off to care for ill family members is becoming quite common among leading nonfederal employers. In our report comparing federal and nonfederal work/family programs, we found that most of the nonfederal organizations we visited permitted employees to use all or a portion of their paid sick leave to care for family members who were ill. Other approaches to this issue some employers used included providing separate "family emergency" leave allowances and combining vacation and sick time into one account to give employees the flexibility to take time off for any reason.

A December 1993 report by the Bureau of National Affairs[4] on a survey of 155 employers of varying sizes and industries confirmed our findings that many organizations allow employees to use sick leave for family members' illnesses. According to the report, 45 percent of the employers allowed salaried employees to use sick leave to care for a sick child; 32 percent allowed sick leave for care of an elderly relative; and 39 percent allowed sick leave for care of other family members.

Expanding the circumstances in which employees may use sick leave can increase their absences from work. Also, if employees substitute sick leave for annual leave they now may be taking to care for ill family members, their lump-sum payments for unused annual leave could be larger when they separate from federal service. Like annual leave sharing, the proposed sick leave amendment could also increase federal salary outlays in cases where employees would have otherwise used unpaid leave to care for ill family members.

Any costs resulting from an increase in the use of paid sick leave could be eventually offset, in part, by reduced retirement system costs. Retiring employees covered by the Civil Service Retirement System may count unused sick leave as service credits in the calculation of their retirement benefits. To the extent that greater amounts of sick leave are used to tend to family members' medical needs, fewer service credits would be available in the retirement benefit calculations. Employees retiring under the Federal Employees Retirement System do not receive service credits for unused sick leave.

As with the annual leave sharing proposal, the effect of the sick leave change on government costs should be examined during the 3-year experiment.

CONCLUSION

Within the overall context of federal employment policies, the changes proposed by H.R. 4361 are, perhaps, relatively minor. They do not, for example, change the amount of annual and sick leave employees accrue each year. Yet, by allowing employees more options for using their leave, this legislation should go a long way toward helping many employees better manage their work, personal, and family responsibilities.

Ms. NORTON. Thank you very much, Mr. Bowling.

Let me try to sort out some of the issues that were raised in the prior testimony by Ms. Green. The notion of sick leave is easier to see and deal with. The notion that a spouse, for example, with a spouse working for the Government is put in an advantaged position over the majority, clearly, who have no such relative working for the Federal Government, has been raised. How do you respond to that notion?

Mr. BOWLING. We do not see that the provision would disadvantage anyone. No one loses anything by it. All it does is allow the employees who are faced with the very real difficulties and challenges of caring for family situations increased flexibility. Therefore, we see that it fits the purpose of the bill.

[4] Bureau of National Affairs, *Paid Leave for Illness and Personal Circumstances*, Personnel Policies Forum Survey No. 151. Washington, D.C.: Bureau of National Affairs, Inc., 1993.

Ms. NORTON. Well, isn't there more than flexibility that comes? Doesn't one end up with more annual leave for the family than the same employee would have if the spouse worked for IBM?

Mr. BOWLING. The family would have together, jointly, the same amount of annual leave. It would just be a question of how they shared it.

I don't think we know enough about what other employers are doing in that sphere to really draw comparisons about who is doing better or worse, but the fact of the matter is that any couple has a set amount of annual leave to deal with between them for the year, and this would not increase that in any way.

Ms. NORTON. Of course Ms. Green says that, given that very fact, they could and perhaps should be encouraged to make more equitable use of their annual leave as they go along. You have to apply for annual leave in advance. Is that not the case?

Mr. BOWLING. You are supposed to have that approved by your supervisor, that is correct.

Ms. NORTON. So what is to keep this couple from simply making the advance determination rather than letting one spouse use up all the annual leave that she has?

Mr. BOWLING. I think the most likely scenario would be that if, for example, one family member had less flexible job responsibilities and couldn't take off as easily, then the one who could take off would use more of their annual leave in caring for their children or dealing with snow days, as you suggested earlier; this provision would simply be used to balance the inequities that might have arisen between the two. It would allow them, for example, to take a family vacation, whereas under the other scenario that I sketched out, they might not be able to. And, as I say, it doesn't increase the amount of annual leave that the Government is paying for.

Ms. NORTON. Do you know of similar provisions being used—widely used in the private sector? Is this very unusual? In other words, increasingly we have two-parent families or at least two spouses working for the same employer because now women are so largely in the work force. How common is what you are advocating for annual leave done in the private sector?

Mr. BOWLING. We don't really know very much about that, frankly. We have found that for sick leave use in the private sector, there is a variety of vehicles in place. In fact, there are many organizations in the private sector that actually go beyond the current OPM regulations that have been proposed.

So there is precedence for more flexible, more generous use of leave in the private sector. How widespread it is, we don't know, but we are aware that the leading organizations that we have looked at do, in fact, offer some opportunities not currently available to the Federal employee.

Ms. NORTON. Of the annual leave variety.

Mr. BOWLING. Of the sick leave variety. We have not been able to come to grips with the issue of annual leave yet because there is such a variety of different packages available.

Ms. NORTON. Yes.

In your testimony you indicate you won't know until you try it and of course we have had good results from GAO investigation of trials, and we ourselves have enacted legislation based on those trials, but if you won't know until you try it, how do you respond to OPM's suggestion, we will try what they are saying? They have reached it on a fairly scientific basis. They say give everybody 5 days. Should we try that, or should we try the more open-ended approach?

Mr. BOWLING. Well, I guess you could look at it either way and make a reasonable argument. However, when you evaluate the risks of the broader proposal in your legislation, it would appear that they aren't very great.

We do not see any likelihood that this will be a costly program, and we don't really anticipate that it is likely to be abused, though we can't really predict that in advance.

Therefore, it seems to us that in light of the relatively minor risks, it would make more sense to go with a somewhat broader approach to begin with for the experiment and then, depending on what the experiment shows, add restrictions or decrease the flexibility if that seemed to be necessary.

Ms. NORTON. That sounds very intelligent to me. For example, if we went only 5 days and we find that people use the 5 days, we won't know anything.

Ms. BOWLING. Exactly.

Ms. NORTON. We won't know if they would have used more and they only used the 5 days because they just couldn't and so they had to do the best they could. We won't even know much if they use 3 days because all we will know is, they couldn't use but 5, and therefore they used less than 5.

Mr. BOWLING. Exactly.

Ms. NORTON. We have had some discussion, as you heard, in the last colloquy with OPM on the definition of family members. In our examination of the programs of other employers, allowing the use of sick leave for family illness, what kinds of definitions did you find were most often used for family members?

Mr. BOWLING. We found in our review of the BNA survey, looking at the four employers' programs that have this type of provision, that in all four cases the definitions were, in fact, somewhat broader than the definition in OPM's regulation. So there is precedent for having the type of definition now in the Leave Sharing Act of 1988, as you mentioned earlier.

Ms. NORTON. I must say, OPM says child, spouse, and parent. The broader definition is spouse—let me see, children, including adopted children. God, does OPM not include adopted children? I have to assume that child includes adopted children—parents, brothers, and sisters, and spouses—their spouse.

Mr. BOWLING. OPM does not include brothers and sisters in this definition.

Ms. NORTON. That is in the 5 CFR.

Mr. BOWLING. And in the current bill.

Ms. NORTON. I don't know how OPM arrived at—my bill simply took from their leave sharing regulations—and they have spouse and parents, children, including adopted children, and spouses.

Mr. BOWLING. But not siblings.

Ms. NORTON. Yes. I am referring to the leave sharing. When you were correcting me, you were looking at their——

Mr. BOWLING. Their regulations.

Ms. NORTON. Their regulations. I am looking at, and, frankly, having a lot of trouble figuring out why they have one set of regulations that use one set of family members, then another set of regulations that define "family member" differently, and what I am using is from their leave sharing regulations.

Mr. BOWLING. You are correct. That does include siblings. Their proposed regulation does not.

Ms. NORTON. Yes; brothers, sisters, and spouses that have individuals related by blood or affinity whose close association with the employee is equivalent of a family relationship. I mean this is fairly broad. Do you think it is too broad?

Mr. BOWLING. That is a policy issue. But, I think that since we are starting with an experimental program based on a 3-year period where corrections could be made if we find it doesn't work out the way we want it or it has unintended consequences, it would seem that starting from a broader definition that is consistent with the Leave Sharing Act of 1988 would make some sense.

Ms. NORTON. In other words, start with the broad and then come back on in if necessary.

Mr. BOWLING. Yes; I think that argument could be made. Again, we do not see a major likelihood of large, costly expenditures on this, so I am not sure the risk of trying that would be too great, and it is consistent with the Leave Sharing Act of 1988, as you have pointed out.

Ms. NORTON. What is your response to OPM's concern with downsizing, they could be left uncovered if these regulations were written broadly, I mean, if this matter was construed broadly?

Mr. BOWLING. Well, it does seem like the issue of coverage is perhaps somewhat greater in losing 252,000 employees than it would be in losing a few more sick days. So I suppose that would be the more urgent question.

Ms. NORTON. I am particularly interested, finally, in State government policies on sick leave and annual leave because it looks like at least on sick leave they are ahead of us. I am not sure of where they are on annual or annual type leave. But I was surprised at that number, 46 States. Could you expand on that please?

Mr. BOWLING. Are you referring now to the OPM statement?

Ms. NORTON. No; I am referring to the 46—what I am referring to—to be specific, is that, yes, OPM found that 46 State governments allow the use of sick leave for family illnesses. How did they get out in front of the Federal Government on this, and what is the experience you believe that has set so many of the States, so many of whom are normally far more conservative in their benefit packages than the Federal Government—what has set them out on this course?

Mr. BOWLING. Well, we are not really sure. We haven't reviewed that study. What we can speak to is the fact that in our review of employers, we did find that among State, county, and private employers, they were examples where they were out in front of the Federal Government. I don't know how prevalent that is, but they seem in some cases to have moved ahead of where the Federal Government is.

Ms. NORTON. Thank you very much, Mr. Bowling. Your testimony and the work you have done has been very instructive and very useful for us.

Mr. BOWLING. Thank you very much.

Ms. NORTON. I would like to call the next witnesses, the final witnesses, a panel of Federal employee organizations: Robert Harnage, national secretary-treasurer, American Federation of Government Employees; Sheila Velazco, president, National Federation of Federal Employees; Susan Shaw, legislative liaison, National Treasury Employees Union; Carolyn Kroon, president, Federally Employed Women.

You may proceed in any order you feel comfortable with.

STATEMENTS OF ROBERT HARNAGE, NATIONAL SECRETARY-TREASURER, AMERICAN FEDERATION OF GOVERNMENT EMPLOYEES; SHEILA VELAZCO, PRESIDENT, NATIONAL FEDERATION OF FEDERAL EMPLOYEES; SUSAN SHAW, LEGISLATIVE LIAISON, NATIONAL TREASURY EMPLOYEES UNION; AND CAROLYN KROON, PRESIDENT, FEDERALLY EMPLOYED WOMEN

Mr. HARNAGE. Madam Chair and members of the subcommittee, my name is Bobby Harnage, and I am the national secretary-treasurer of the American Federation of Government Employees, AFL–CIO.

On behalf of the more than 700 Federal employees and District of Columbia employees our union represents, I thank you for the opportunity to testify here today in support of H.R. 4361, the Federal Employees Family Friendly Leave Act. I also want to commend you, Madam Chair, for your leadership on this issue and dozens more concerning Federal employees and the retirees.

AFGE strongly supports both of the major provisions of the Federal Employees Family Friendly Leave Act. Allowing Federal employees to use their accumulated sick leave to care for relatives who are ill and allowing transfers of accumulated annual leave to family members who are also Federal employees is long overdue.

The obvious rationale is that the policy will relieve some of the burden of balancing the demands of one's job and one's family obligations, but more important is the recognition that leave is a form of earned compensation that belongs to the employee.

It has been humiliation for a responsible adult who happens to be a Federal employee to have to evade the truth in using sick leave to care for family members. Let us be honest. Balancing work and family needs is not something that has only emerged in the last decade. Children, spouses, and elderly parents have always gotten sick, and as responsible adults Federal employees have probably always used their own sick leave in order to provide care to their relatives when it has been needed. That such laudable and responsible behavior has had to take place under the shroud of secrecy and deceit is both demeaning and without good purpose.

The Office of Personnel Management, this week, issued a proposed regulation allowing Federal employees to use a maximum of 5 days per year to care for an ill relative. OPM explains the 5-day limit as having been put in place to ensure that employees have adequate sick leave to meet their own needs as well as those of their family. AFGE does not believe these limitations are necessary.

The National Performance Review recommendations on reinventing Government proposed that the Government cease treating its employees as arrogant children whose use of time needed to be closely monitored. The NPR went on to argue that trusting employees to use their own best judgment in such areas as scheduling of their work days would bolster morale and encourage employees to do their best work. AFGE is pleased that OPM has recognized that the Federal Government's leave policy needs to be changed, and we view their proposal as a positive first step.

Like most adults who regularly meet their obligations to both their jobs and their families, Federal employees have vast experience in budgeting their time and money among numerous competing demands. If Federal employees need 6 of their 13 sick days to take care of sick children, should they really have to lie about it to their supervisors? We think not. AFGE therefore supports the provisions of the Family Friendly Leave Act because it leaves decisions on the allocation of sick leave to the Federal employee, the person who is in the best position to judge who needs care on any of those 13 days of sick leave he has earned.

The Family Friendly Leave Act also proposes allowing Federal employees to transfer unused annual leave to a family member who is also a Federal employee. AFGE also strongly supports this provision. Again, this provision recognizes that leave is a form of earned compensation, the use of which should be controlled by its owner. There are numerous instances where family members may jointly decide that it is preferable for one individual rather than another to be off work. The transfer would allow family members to decide how to budget their household assets broadly defined to include accumulation of paid leave.

AFGE applauds the bill's relative lack of restrictions on either the use of sick leave to care for sick relatives or the transfer of annual leave between family members. We feel certain that Federal employees will not abuse these expanded rights and will appreciate being treated as adults capable of making their own decisions. We also believe that these rather modest changes will enhance the Government's ability to continue to attract and retain high quality Federal employees.

This concludes my testimony, and if you have any questions, I will be happy to respond.

[The prepared statement of Mr. Harnage follows:]

PREPARED STATEMENT OF ROBERT HARNAGE, NATIONAL SECRETARY-TREASURER, AMERICAN FEDERATION OF GOVERNMENT EMPLOYEES

Madam Chair and members of the Subcommittee: My name is Bobby Harnage, and I am the National Secretary-Treasurer of the American Federation of Government Employees, AFL–CIO. On behalf of the more than 700,000 Federal and District of Columbia employees our union represents, I thank you for the opportunity to testify here today in support of H.R. 4361, the Federal Employees Family Friendly Leave Act. I also want to commend you, Madam Chair, for your leadership on this issue and dozens more concerning Federal employees and retirees.

AFGE strongly supports both of the major provisions of the Federal Employees Family Friendly Leave Act. Allowing Federal Employees to use their accumulated sick leave to care for relatives who are ill, and allowing transfers of accumulated annual leave to family members who are also Federal employees is long overdue. The obvious rationale is that the policy will relieve some of the burden of balancing the demands of one's job and one's family obligations. But more important, it is a recognition that leave is a form of earned compensation that belongs to the employee.

It has been humiliating for a responsible adult who happens to be a Federal employee to have to evade the truth when using sick leave to care for family members. Let us be honest: Balancing work and family needs is not something that has only emerged in the last decade. Children, spouses, and elderly parents have always gotten sick. And as responsible adults, Federal employees have probably always used their own sick leave in order to provide care to their relatives when it has been needed. That such laudable and responsible behavior has had to take place under the shroud of secrecy and deceit is both demeaning and without good purpose.

The Office of Personnel Management this week issued a proposed regulation allowing Federal employees to use a maximum of 5 days per year to care for an ill relative. OPM explains the 5-day limit as having been put in place "to ensure that employees have adequate sick leave to meet their own needs as well as those of their families." AFGE does not believe these limitations are necessary. The National Performance Reviews recommendations on reinventing Government propose that the Government cease treating its employees as "errant children" whose use of time needed to be closely monitored. The NPR went on to argue that trusting employees to use their own best judgment in such areas as the scheduling of their work days would bolster morale and encourage people to do their best work.

AFGE is pleased that OPM has recognized that the Federal Government's leave policy needs to be changed, and we view their proposal as a positive first step. Like most adults who regularly meet their obligations to both their jobs and their families, Federal employees have vast experience in budgeting their time and money among numerous competing demands. If Federal employees needs 6 of their 13 sick days to take care of sick children, should they really have to lie about it to their supervisors? We think not.

AFGE therefore supports the provisions of the Family Friendly Leave Act, because it leaves decisions on the allocation of sick leave to the Federal employee, the person who is in the best position to judge who needs care on any of those 13 days of sick leave he has earned.

The Family Friendly Leave Act also proposes allowing Federal employees to transfer unused annual leave to a family member who is also a Federal employee. AFGE also strongly supports this provision. Again, this provision recognizes that leave is a form of earned compensation, the use of which should be controlled by its owner. There are numerous instances where family members may jointly decide that it is preferable for one individual rather than another to be off work. The transfers would allow family members to decide how to budget their household's assets, broadly defined to include accumulations of paid leave.

AFGE applauds the bill's relative lack of restrictions on either the use of sick leave to care for sick relatives or the transfers of annual leave between family members. We feel certain that Federal employees will not abuse these expanded rights, and will appreciate being treated as adults capable of making their own decisions. We also believe that these rather modest changes will enhance the Government's ability to continue to attract and retain a high-quality Federal workforce.

Ms. NORTON. Could we have the next person to testify?

Ms. VELAZCO. Good afternoon. I am pleased to be here, and I want to say first of all, Madam Chairwoman, I appreciate your efforts and the committee's efforts in H.R. 4361 to accommodate the special needs of today's work culture, a culture made up of individuals who are often single parents or households that include both parents working, extended families, or the sandwiched generation, those of us who have elderly parents as well as children to care for.

I would like to not actually read my comments but, rather, have them just submitted into the record and just address a couple of concerns.

The two areas I would like to address are, first of all, the definition of a family member, and second, the scope of the annual leave transfer. While I am pleased that OPM said today that they are willing to consider opening up their definition, very narrow definition in this instance, of what a family member is, I think it is essential that we agree on a much broader definition, a definition which must include and take into consideration what today's families really are, and I would like to offer some personal experience that I don't think is unique—I think it is replicated throughout the country—but under OPM's definition it would not have allowed a person to use this annual leave.

When I was young, I was the last of nine children, and when my sister and I were still very young girls, my mother died, my father was ill and unable to care for us, so an older sister took us in, took care of us through the time we graduated from high school. Under these circumstances, under the definition of OPM, that person would not be allowed to use any of their sick leave.

I think that that is not a unique situation. We have extended families, we have foster care children, we have people who live together that care for each other that are not related, and I think it is essential that we broaden the definition.

The other concern I have is on the scope of the Leave Transfer Program for annual leave. While I think it is a very important step forward, again, I am very practical and I think that we should look at realities today in our work force. I know of two families who were burned out of homes that would not meet this annual leave transfer. They didn't have anybody in our offices who worked for the Federal Government, and yet they had emergency situations which the rest of us would have been glad to donate annual leave to. So I would like to have it considered that we broaden the scope of the recipients of annual leave transfers and maybe include circumstances in that also.

That concludes my remarks, and I would be glad to take any questions.

[The prepared statement of Ms. Velazco follows:]

PREPARED STATEMENT OF SHEILA VELAZCO, PRESIDENT, NATIONAL FEDERATION OF FEDERAL EMPLOYEES

Good morning, Madam Chair and Members of the Subcommittee, on behalf of the National Federation of Federal Employees, I am pleased to be here to offer our views on H.R. 4361, the Federal Employees Family Friendly Leave Act. NFFE is the nation's oldest union of federal employees, representing the interests of nearly 150,000 federal employees and their families in over 50 agencies throughout the federal government.

NFFE supports the goal of making the federal workplace more family friendly. NFFE believes that in order to maintain its status as a model employer, the federal government must continue to strive to remain a healthy and humane workplace. If we are serious about improving the performance of the federal work force and relying on every worker for valuable ideas, it is imperative that we create a workplace culture in which employees are unencumbered by family care concerns that distract employees from performing at their peak.

These views were echoed in the report of the National Performance Review which held that the "government's ability to recruit and retain the best employees—and to motivate them to be productive—depends on its ability to create a satisfying work environment." There is ample evidence in the private sector to support this claim. For example, Johnson & Johnson, Inc., reported that its employees who used flextime and family leave were absent 50 percent fewer days than its regular work force. Moreover, 71 percent of those workers using benefits said the policies were "very important" to their decision to stay with the company.

H.R. 4361's goal of making the federal government more "family friendly" through changes in the current policies governing the use of sick and annual leave is timely and just. And the offerings of flextime, part-time, leave-sharing, and unpaid family and medical leave each play an important role in helping federal employees balance their personal and professional responsibilities.

However, even with these current policies in place, federal workers still encounter problems—chiefly flexible work policies which are not implemented fully in many agencies. For example, the National Performance Review found that only 53 percent of employees with dependent care needs believe their agencies understand and support family issues. Thirty-eight percent indicated that their agencies do not provide the full range of dependent-care services available. NFFE believes that while adoption of the changes contained in H.R. 4361 is an important component in creating the family-friendly work environment, measures should also be put in place to ensure that current policies are followed.

Additionally, NFFE has concerns about how the term "family member", as it applies to use of sick leave, will be defined under H.R. 4361. As the subcommittee is aware, last week the Office of Personnel Management proposed regulations which would allow employees to use five days of sick leave to care for family members. On first examination, these regulations would seem to fulfill the goals of section 2 of H.R. 4361. Unfortunately however, OPM's regulations very narrowly define family member as either a parent, spouse, or child. NFFE believes that the extremely narrow definition of family member in the OPM regulation represents a serious obstacle to achieving the goal of a family friendly workplace. In today's society, the compact nuclear family of the past is fading. The modern family is often an extended family which can include those not related by blood or by law. NFFE believes that if the goal of creating a more family-friendly workplace is to be reached, then the definition of family member should be one that accurately reflects the realities of today's modern society.

In addition, under OPM's proposed regulations, employees would only be allowed to use five sick days a year to care for family members. NFFE believes that in some cases this five-day limit may be inadequate. Federal employees should have the option of using additional sick leave days to care for family members.

Finally, NFFE supports the concept of leave transfers between relatives as provided for in Section 3 of H.R. 4361. But why limit these benefits to federal employees who are related? If one employee is willing to transfer some of his or her annual leave directly to another federal employee, why should it matter if they are or are not related? NFFE believes expansion of this provision, to allow for leave transfers between all federal employees, will create not only a family-friendly workplace, but also a worker friendly workplace with heightened morale.

In conclusion, NFFE is thankful for the efforts the members of this subcommittee have made in creating a workplace that is more responsive to the needs of its employees.

Ms. SHAW. Madam Chairwoman, Mrs. Morella, I am Susan Shaw. I am the assistant director of legislation for the National Treasury Employees Union. I am pleased to present testimony today on H.R. 4361, the Federal Employees Family Friendly Leave Act.

While NTEU supports the Office of Personnel Management's recently proposed regulations allowing up to 5 days of sick leave each year to care for a child, spouse, or parent, H.R. 4361 goes even further to strengthen the important protections for working men and women attempting to care for their loved ones.

As evidenced by OPM's concurrence that other recently implemented leave-sharing programs have provided significant benefit to the Federal Government, even further gains can be expected from the passage of H.R. 4361, not the least of which is in terms of attracting and retaining quality employees.

Your bill provides for an employee of the Federal Government to use sick leave to give care or otherwise attend to the medical needs of a family member, and we are particularly supportive of your provision to allow employees to transfer annual leave between family members even in the absence of any medical emergency. NTEU strongly believes that Federal employees should be able to address their health care needs and care for their infirm family members without fear of losing their jobs.

As the Congress continues to explore ways to reinvent Government, it becomes increasingly important that every effort be made to retain a quality work force. Legislation such as the Federal Employees Family Friendly Leave Act takes us closer to achieving that goal, and we strongly support it.

That concludes my statement, and I too would be happy to answer any questions.

[The prepared statement of Mr. Tobias follows:]

PREPARED STATEMENT OF ROBERT M. TOBIAS, PRESIDENT, NATIONAL TREASURY EMPLOYEES UNION

Madam Chairwoman, Members of the Subcommittee, on behalf of the over 150,000 members of the National Treasury Employees Union (NTEU), I am pleased to present testimony today on H.R. 4361, the Federal Employees Family Friendly Leave Act. While NTEU supports the Office of Personnel Management's (OPM) recently proposed regulations allowing up to five days of sick leave each year to care for a child, spouse, or parent, H.R. 4361 goes even further to strengthen the important protections for working men and women attempting to care for their loved ones.

I wish to thank you, Madam Chairwoman, for introducing and taking action on this humane piece of legislation. Studies have consistently shown that employer programs that assist employees in balancing their work and family responsibilities reap important dividends for the employer. As evidenced by OPM's concurrence that other recently implemented leave sharing programs have provided significant benefit to the federal government, even further gains can be expected from the passage of such "family friendly" legislation as H.R. 4361, not the least of which is in terms of attracting and retaining quality employees. I commend the Subcommittee's leadership on this and so many other issues of importance to federal employees and retirees, and I appreciate the invitation to testify at today's hearing.

Anyone who is a parent knows all too well the difficulties in providing competent and dependable care for their children, especially during the initial stages of a child's life. Anyone who has a aging parent with medical problems can appreciate the difficulty in dealing with work demands and the care of a parent. In fact, many of our members and a large cross section of the federal work force belong to what is sometimes referred to as the "sandwich" generation which must care for young children as well as elderly parents. The stress involved in this responsibility oftentimes affects an employee's work performance.

H.R. 4361 provides for a three year demonstration project whereby an employee of the Federal Government may use sick leave to give care or otherwise attend to the medical needs of a family member. The legislation also modifies the voluntary leave transfer program with respect to employees who are members of the same family, allowing the transfer of annual leave from one employee to another federal worker who is a family member of the employee, even in the absence of any medical emergency. No later than six months prior to the end of the three year demonstration, OPM is required to submit a report to the Congress evaluating the operation of the program and making recommendations as to whether or not it should be continued beyond the sunset date.

As the Subcommittee is well aware, to important pieces of federal employee leave legislation were signed into law last year after years of deadlock before the Congress. The landmark Family and Medical Leave Act and the Federal Employee Leave Sharing Act reauthorized last year are important federal employee benefits that offer some degree of income protection. NTEU continues to be very supportive of measures to improve and expand the federal leave sharing program, and supports H.R. 4631 to the extent that it builds on this effort.

Recalling testimony before the Subcommittee last year on reauthorization of the leave sharing program, many of the recommendations encouraging expansion of the program by NTEU and other have been incorporated into H.R. 4631. NTEU applauds the consideration the Subcommittee is giving to this issue.

NTEU strongly believes that federal employees should be able to address their health care needs and care for their infirm family members without fear of losing their jobs. As the Congress continues to explore ways to reinvent government, it becomes increasingly important that every effort be made to retain a quality federal work force. Legislation such as the Federal Employee Family Friendly Leave Act takes us closer to achieving that goal.

Again, I appreciate the opportunity to present the views of NTEU here today, and I will be happy to answer any questions you might have.

Ms. KROON. Madam Chair, Congresswoman Morella, I am Carolyn Kroon, president of Federally Employed Women. FEW is a nonprofit, nonpartisan membership organization representing over 1 million women employed by the Federal Government throughout the world.

FEW is pleased to be afforded this opportunity to testify before this subcommittee and on your efforts, Madam Chair, to implement family friendly leave policies in the Federal workplace. H.R. 4361 would make important changes in the use of sick leave and expand the opportunity to transfer annual leave to family members. These things would be welcomed by millions of Federal workers.

For nearly 20 years the demographic profile of the American workplace has reflected increasing diversity. With women making up nearly half of the American labor force, two-parent working families and single-parent families have stormed the gates of American business and the Federal Government.

According to the OPM, women comprise 43 percent of the total civilian nonpostal work force. In addition to childbearing and childrearing responsibilities, OPM has estimated that more than a quarter of Federal workers, 572,000 out of 2,200,000, were expected to have elder care responsibilities during the 5 years from 1991 to 1996.

Managers from the private and public sector have had to develop programs which recognize the need to balance competing work and family responsibilities. These changes were not made for altruistic reasons, they made good business sense.

A 1991 report by the Merit Systems Protection Board found that the Government lagged behind both what many other major employers provided and what many employees needed. More relevant to today's hearing, MSPB went further in making a formal recommendation that the Government consider changing its sick leave regulations to permit employees to use some of their sick leave for sick and elderly dependents. With the introduction of the Federal Employees Family Friendly Leave Act and the recent OPM proposed regulations on expanded use of sick leave, FEW believes the time to turn principle into practice is upon us.

Although there seems to be unanimous agreement that the Government could and should do more in the way of developing, implementing, and encouraging the use of family friendly programs, there is apparent disagreement on how to proceed. FEW has been a long-time supporter of expanding the use of sick leave for family purposes. The current policy is inadequate in providing the flexibility that workers need to uphold their family responsibilities and has spawned inherent difficulties and inconsistencies in practice.

For example, under the current system, a parent could use his or her sick leave to care for a child with chickenpox, but if that same child was injured in an accident and has to be hospitalized, the employee would have to turn to alternate paid or unpaid leave.

With the implementation of the Family Medical Leave Act of 1993, it made even less sense to suggest that an employee can have guaranteed access to leave without pay for family caretaking purposes but that that same access to his or her own paid sick leave is denied.

Efforts to limit the use of sick leave for family purposes, such as OPM's proposed regulation to allow 5 days of sick leave for family use per year, are insufficient and would be difficult to administer. A 5-day period would not accommodate a serious illness or accident and would require the tracking of two different types of sick leave. Although recognized as better than the current system, incremental steps are not enough and should be avoided.

In addition, H.R. 4361 includes a broad definition of "family member" that is consistent with the terminology used in the now permanent Federal Employees Leave Sharing Program. This definition is more accommodating to the needs of a wide variety of family compositions than the definition contained in the OPM proposal. The OPM proposal goes further, however, in enabling employees to use sick leave for purposes of bereavement. FEW would encourage the inclusion of this provision in H.R. 4361 to ensure that the legislation comprehensively addresses the expansion of sick leave use.

The Federal Employees Family Friendly Leave Act would also enable Federal workers to have the opportunity to transfer annual leave to family members. FEW understands that this proposal is not designed to further accommodate for medical emergencies but to ensure that families also take personal time off for vacation, training opportunities, et cetera.

The inability to use sick leave for family purposes has created a situation where parents have small annual leave balances. According to OPM's 1992 survey of Federal employees, 51 percent have used annual leave to attend to a family member's illness or medicare. The notion of transferred annual leave makes practical sense, and the legislation has built-in safeguards that ensure that the leave is used for such purposes.

If there is one area which leaves room for improvement in the legislative proposal before us, it is the limited 3-year effective date. Although other initiatives such as the leave sharing program were implemented as pilot projects, there is a wealth of evidence which supports the permanent installation of these policies now. With reinventing Government initiatives changing the Federal labor-management relationship, eliminating cumbersome procedures and duplication, imposing personnel reductions and decentralizing personnel policy, a firm commitment to the accommodation of family friendly programs is necessary. The message must come from the top, and it must be loud and clear in order to ensure that it trickles down to every rung of the management ladder.

FEW applauds your efforts, Madam Chair, to take the lead in ensuring timely implementation of family friendly leave policies in the Federal sector. H.R. 4361 would greatly expand the use of existing leave programs and in that regard may be seen as too much too soon. Others may contend that there is difficulty in promoting progressive policies that benefit only those employees who have families or, more specifically, families who are also federally employed. The criticism may simply be a smoke screen to thwart change.

The fact that most Federal workers have family responsibilities may not come as a surprise. However, according to a national study conducted by the Family and Work Institute, that figure may be far larger than imagined; 87 percent of workers live with family members; 47 percent care for dependents, children, ill spouses, or partners or elders. Family friendly leave programs should be seen as a benefit to not just a few but to all Federal workers.

I believe that the Federal Government can adopt a model employer orientation and develop sound and progressive family friendly policies which do not conflict with its primary duty to accomplish its mission in a fiscally responsible way. I also believe the change would be welcomed by Federal workers and would greatly improve the Federal Government's ability to recruit and retain a highly qualified, productive, and motivated work force.

This concludes my prepared statement, Madam Chair, and I will be happy to answer any questions.

[The prepared statement of Ms. Kroon follows:]

PREPARED STATEMENT OF CAROLYN KROON, PRESIDENT, FEDERALLY EMPLOYED WOMEN

Madame Chair and distinguished members of the Subcommittee, I am Carolyn Kroon, President, Federally Employed Women [FEW]. FEW is a non-profit, non-partisan membership organization representing over one million women employed by the Federal government throughout the world. Founded in 1968, FEW has actively worked to eliminate sex discrimination and enhance career potential for civilian and military women working in the federal sector.

FEW is pleased to be afforded this opportunity to testify before the House Post Office and Civil Service Subcommittee on Compensation and Employee Benefits on your efforts, Madame Chair, to implement family friendly leave policy in the federal workplace. H.R. 4361 would make important changes in the use of sick leave and expand the opportunity to transfer annual leave to family members. These changes would be welcomed by millions of federal workers.

DEMOGRAPHIC CHANGES PROMPT ATTENTION TO FAMILY RESPONSIBILITIES

For nearly twenty years, the demographic profile of the American workplace has reflected increasing diversity. With women making up nearly half of the American labor force, two-parent working families and single parent families have stormed the gates of American businesses. According to the Bureau of Labor Statistics, the number of mothers in the paid labor force is at an all time high 67 percent. In addition, 54 percent of working mothers have children under three years of age.[1]

A similar change has taken place in the federal sector. According to the Office of Personnel Management [OPM], women comprise 43 percent of the federal civilian non-postal workforce today. The percentage of women has consistently risen over the past thirty years, making up approximately 29 percent of the federal civilian workforce in 1960, 31 percent in 1970, and 39 percent in 1980. In addition to childbearing and child rearing responsibilities, OPM has estimated that more than a quarter of federal workers—570,000 out of 2.2 million—were expected to have eldercare responsibilities during the five years from 1991 to 1996.[2]

Managers from the private and public sectors have had to adjust personnel policies that were modeled after the "nuclear family" of the 1950s by developing programs which recognize the need to balance competing work and family responsibilities. These changes were not made for altruistic reasons; on the contrary, they made good business sense. Research indicates that workers who feel supported by "workplace cultures that are more accommodating of personal and family needs feel less burned out by work, are more loyal to their employers, are more willing to work hard to help their companies succeed, and are more satisfied with their jobs."[3] These factors no doubt heavily impact workplace productivity and tenure.

Over the past five years, numerous sources have recommended that the Federal government increase its use of family friendly programs. In addition to deficiencies levied by federal labor unions, professional associations, and women's organizations, the Merit Systems Protection Board [MSPB] found the government "lagging behind both what many other major employers provide and what many employees need."

[1] U.S. Department of Labor, Bureau of Labor Statistics, 1992.

[2] *Federal Times*, "Taking Care of Mom and Dad Puts Demands on Workers," May 31, 1993

[3] "The Changing Workforce: Highlights of the National Study," New York: Families and Work Institute, No. 1, 1993.

More relevant to today's hearing, MSPB went further in making a formal recommendation that the government "consider changing its sick leave regulations to permit employees to use some of their sick leave for sick or elderly dependents."[4]

The General Accounting Office subsequently recommended that OPM "play a stronger leadership role in dealing with federal sector work/family issues."[5] Even OPM has been critical of the federal leave system suggesting that it "provides the least benefit to employees with the least amount of service, thus limiting its usefulness to many employees with child care needs."[6]

Recognizing that the Federal government is the largest single employer in the country, the MSPB and the GAO encouraged the government to adopt a "model employer" orientation and develop family friendly programs accordingly. To that end, some progress has been made to date.

Today, federal employees and managers can turn to OPM's Work and Family Center for information and assistance. Thanks to Congressional initiatives, the Federal government has implemented policies which promote flexible work schedules, job sharing, use of sick leave for adoption purposes, leave sharing programs, and more recently family and medical leave. The National Performance Review suggests that the Administration is firmly committed to such policies, including the use of sick leave to care for sick or elderly dependents."[7]

For years, FEW has joined this chorus for change. With the introduction of the Federal Employees Family Friendly Leave Act and the recent OPM proposed regulations on expanded use of sick leave, the time to turn principles into practice is upon us.

EXPANSION OF SICK LEAVE FOR FAMILY PURPOSES

Although there seems to be unanimous agreement that the government could and should do more in the way of developing, implementing, and encouraging the use of family friendly programs, there is apparent disagreement on how to proceed.

Currently, federal personnel policy provides sick leave with full pay when an employee is incapacitated for duty; is receiving medical, dental, or optical examination or treatment; is required to give care and attendance to a family member afflicted with a contagious disease; or would jeopardize the health of others because of exposure to a contagious disease.[8]

FEW has been a long-time supporter of expanding the use of sick leave for family purposes. The current policy is inadequate in providing the flexibility that workers need to uphold their family responsibilities and has spawned inherent difficulties and inconsistencies in practice. For example, under the current system, a parent could use his/her sick leave to care for a child with the chicken pox, but if that same child was injured in an accident and had to be hospitalized, the employee would have to turn to alternative paid or unpaid leave. With the implementation of the Family and Medical Leave Act of 1993, it makes even less sense to suggest that an employee can have guaranteed access to leave without pay for family caretaking purposes but not that same access to his/her own paid sick leave.

Efforts to limit the use of sick leave for family purposes—such as the OPM proposed regulations to allow five days of sick leave for family use per year[9]—are insufficient and would be difficult to administer. A five day period would not accommodate a serious illness or accident, would require the tracking of two different types of sick leave, and would send a mixed message to federal workers. Although recognized as better than the current system, incremental steps are not enough and should be avoided.

H.R. 4361 includes a broad definition of family member that is consistent with the terminology used in the now permanent Federal Employee Leave Sharing Program. According to 5 CFR Sec. 630.902, "family member means the following rel-

---

[4] U.S. Merit Systems Protection Board Report: "Balancing Work Responsibilities and Family Needs: The Federal Civil Service Response," Washington, DC: U.S. Government Printing Office, November 1991.

[5] U.S. General Accounting Office Report to Congressional Committees. "The Changing Workforce: Comparison of Federal and Nonfederal Work/Family Programs and Approaches (GAO/GGD–92–84)," Washington, DC: U.S. Government Printing Office, April 1992.

[6] U.S. Office of Personnel Management: "A Study of the Work and Family Needs of the Federal Workforce: A Report to Congress by the Office of Personnel Management," Washington, DC: U.S. Government Printing Office, April 1992.

[7] Report of the National Performance Review. "From Red Tape to Results: Creating a Government That Works Better & Costs Less," Washington, DC: U.S. Government Printing Office, September 7, 1993.

[8] 5 CFR Sec. 630.401.

[9] OPM Proposed Rules were published in the *Federal Register,* Vol. 59, No. 90 on May 11, 1994.

atives of the employee: (a) spouse, and parents, thereof; (b) children, including adopted children, and spouses thereof; (c) parents; (d) brothers and sisters, and spouses thereof; and (e) any individual related by blood or affinity whose close association with the employee is the equivalent of a family relationship." This definition is more accommodating to the needs of a wide variety of family compositions than the definition contained in the OPM proposal.[10]

The OPM proposal goes further, however, in enabling employees to use sick leave for purposes of bereavement. FEW would encourage the inclusion of his provision in H.R. 4361 to ensure that the legislation comprehensively addresses the expansion of sick leave use.

TRANSFER OF ANNUAL LEAVE BETWEEN FAMILY MEMBERS

The Federal Employees Family Friendly Leave Act would also enable federal workers the opportunity to transfer annual leave to family members. FEW understands that this proposal is not designed to allow further accommodations for medical emergencies but to ensure that families can also take personal time off for vacation, training opportunities, etc.

The inability to use sick leave for family purposes has created a situation where parents have small annual leave balances. According to OPM's Survey of Federal Employees, "about half (51%) have used annual leave to tend to family members' illnesses or medical care." [11] The notion of transferring annual leave makes practical sense and the legislation has built-in safeguards that ensure that the leave is used for such purposes. The use of donated annual leave will still have to be scheduled and approved in advance and employees will not get reimbursed for transferred leave in the event they separate from federal service during that same year.

IMPLEMENTING DATE

If there is one area which leaves room for improvement in the legislative proposal before us, it is the limited three-year effective date. Although other initiatives such as the leave sharing programs were implemented as pilot projects, there is a wealth of evidence which supports the permanent installment of these policies now. With reinventing government initiatives changing the federal labor-management relationship, eliminating cumbersome procedures and duplication, imposing personnel reductions, and decentralizing personnel policy, a firm commitment to the accommodation of family friendly programs is necessary. That message must come from the top and it must be loud and clear in order to ensure that it trickles down to every rung of the management ladder.

CONCLUSION

FEW applauds your efforts, Madame Chair, to take the lead in ensuring the timely implementation of family friendly leave policies in the federal sector. H.R. 4361 would greatly expand the use of existing leave programs and in that regard may be seen as too much too soon. Others may contend that there is difficulty in promoting progressive policies that benefit only those employees who have families or, more specifically, families who are also federally employed. That criticism may simply be a smoke screen to thwart change for change sake.

Although women are still maintaining the lion's share of family caretaking responsibilities for children and elderly family members, the lack of child care, eldercare, and long term care policies have meant that flexible work schedules and leave options are welcomed by both male and female workers. The Federal government must overcome any political or philosophical barriers which have thwarted or delayed the implementation of specific family friendly programs or the comprehensive evaluation of the availability and congruence of such programs from a holistic perspective. The traditional piece-meal approach has enabled consistent progress but produced inconsistencies as well.

The fact that most workers have family responsibilities may not come as a surprise, however, according to the Families and Work Institute, that figure may be far larger than imagined: 87% of workers live with family members and 47 percent

---

[10] The OPM regulations use the definition codified by the Family and Medical Leave Act (PL–103–03). That definition was narrowed due to opposition to the private sector standards from the business community. It can be reasonably assumed that a broader definition for federal workers would have been enacted had the legislation solely been directed to the federal sector.

[11] U.S. Office of Personnel Management Special Report: "Survey of Federal Employees," Washington, DC: U.S. Government Printing Office, May 1992.

care for dependents (children, ill spouses or partners, or elders).[12] Family friendly leave programs should, thus, be seen as a benefit to not just a few but to all federal workers.

I believe that the Federal government can adopt a "model employer" orientation and develop sound and progressive family friendly policies which do not conflict with its primary duty—to accomplish its mission in a fiscally responsible way. I also believe that change would be welcomed by federal workers and would greatly improve the Federal government's ability to recruit and retain a highly qualified, productive, and motivated workforce.

Ms. NORTON. Thank you very much.

I would like to turn to Ms. Morella, the ranking member, for such comments as she might want to make or such questions as she might want to ask.

Mrs. MORELLA. Thank you. Thank you, Madam Chair.

I would like to ask unanimous consent that a statement be placed in the record about the bill and in response to some of the testimony that appeared before I arrived.

Ms. NORTON. Without objection, it is so ordered.

Mrs. MORELLA. Thank you.

[The prepared statement of Hon. Constance A. Morella follows:]

PREPARED STATEMENT OF HON. CONSTANCE A. MORELLA, A REPRESENTATIVE IN CONGRESS FROM THE STATE OF MARYLAND

Madam Chair, I am pleased to support H.R. 4361, the Federal Employees Family Friendly Leave Act and commend you for introducing this legislation which will truly be "family friendly". It will undoubtedly help the government to recruit and retain the best into public service and bring benefits available to federal employees more in line with innovative private sector employment situations.

I understand that some people are concerned that this legislation will give a family with two or more federal employees distinct advantage over one which has one family member in federal service. This may give some cause for concern; however, I am sure that there are some measures available in progressive private sector firms which more than compensate their employees. Some instances are: companies which permit conversion of leave from sick leave to vacation leave; companies which offer a cafeteria plan with the ability to trade off one benefit for another when needed. Indeed, government should never hesitate in setting an example to promote family friendly policies, even if there are no private sector firms that offer the same provisions to share leave among family members as proposed by this legislation.

I wholeheartedly agree with GAO's Timothy Bowling, who supports the provision that the program should be tried for three years to determine whether or not it is effective. The cost or savings of the program would be evident by then. I note that Mr. Bowling was before this subcommittee exactly a year ago testifying on the reauthorization of the Federal Employees Leave Sharing Act of 1988. I am pleased that a person of Mr. Bowling's knowledge, caliber, and dedication on this issue is in support of the legislation before us.

I also commend the Office of Personnel Management for publishing their proposed OPM regulations on sick leave in the Federal Register on May 11. However, I believe that Chairman Norton's legislation goes further and is worthy of full consideration. I do have some concern with OPM's testimony and will take the opportunity to ask for clarification at the appropriate time.

I welcome all the witnesses and thank them for their interest in this important measure. I look forward to hearing all the witnesses.

Thank you, Madam Chair.

Mrs. MORELLA. I just want to comment that I couldn't agree more with the people who have testified. I agree that what we need in the Federal Government is more family friendly workplace policies, no doubt about it. In fact, I think the Federal Government should be a model for the private sector.

[12] Families and Work Institute: "The Changing Workforce: A National Survey."

I was most interested in a report that recently came out by the Carnegie Commission dealing with infants through age 3 in terms of what is happening in our society, the importance of the kind of bonding of parents with children, and the fact that we have difficulties with child care.

One of the recommendations of the Carnegie Commission was the fact that we should do more with the Family and Medical Leave Act, that we should expand it further, we should offer more, and that we should even look into paid time for parenting or for illness of a child, and I think that this bill takes a step in that kind of family friendly direction—this bill would allow parents who work for the Federal Government to be able to use their sick leave time to be with members of their family, their children. So I think it moves in the right direction. I wholeheartedly agree with it.

I would agree with what I know you mentioned, Madam Chair, when OPM was testifying, in terms of your critique of their response to the bill; this bill is the one that really does move us in the direction we must go.

So I have no questions unless anybody on the panel—here's your opportunity—to make any statement that you didn't have a chance to make. But I concur, and I thank you very much for appearing before us.

Does anybody have anything they want to say?

I yield back the balance of my time.

Ms. NORTON. I want to thank the ranking member, who has been a leader in matters affecting leave policies in the Federal Government, and I very much appreciate her remarks.

I appreciate as well your reference to chicken pox—that is to say, you can use your sick leave if your child happens to have a contagious disease. I must say, I greet that rather cynically because I believe it may have more to do with protecting us than the child. Otherwise, I can't imagine why contagious diseases would be treated differently from a broken leg, and somehow or the other that has got to be cleared up.

Let me also say that the sunset within 3 years which you also mentioned is related entirely to evaluating the matter so that it could be reauthorized, and that is the way the committee often looks at such programs where it doesn't have enough data to render a final judgment. You will recall we did that on the transit bill as well.

What is your reaction to the OPM objection that that family annual leave sharing may be unfair to employees who do not have relatives employed by the Government, since you represent both kinds of employees?

Ms. KROON. Madam Chair, we feel that they really need to be able to use their annual leave to share.

If you look at the statistics, the survey of Federal employees of May 1992 showed that single parents and dual-income parents make up over 25 percent of the Federal work force, but 12 percent of those people have children under the age of 12, which means you are going to be having accidents and illnesses where you need to be home with your children.

Twelve percent of the entire Federal work force at the time this survey was taken had the responsibility for elder care, and an additional 13 percent said that they anticipated this responsibility for elder care within the next 5 years, which makes up a total of 26 percent of our work force taking care of elder people in their families.

Women make up 43 percent of the Federal work force, and statistics show right now that women spend 18 years of their lives raising their children and 18 years taking care of elderly parents.

Individuals with families have increased burdens and responsibilities, and it just shows that in the private sector studies that have been made—in their studies, excuse me, on private sector workplaces, it shows a dramatic improvement in employee morale, increased productivity, and employee loyalty to that business when they have family friendly policies in the workplace, and I think it just makes good business sense to do this.

Ms. NORTON. Yes, please.

Ms. VELAZCO. Madam Chairwoman, I would like to respond to that. I think most people who work for the Federal Government come to the Federal Government because they have a lot of humanity and caring. I don't think those employees who don't have brothers and sisters, parents, or children will regret that those who do can have time off to care for them.

Ms. NORTON. Thank you.

Now OPM has said look, we are moving ahead on this, we are going to do by regulation 5 days, and their 5 days are related to their own findings, what the data apparently revealed about the use of sick leave by Federal employees. Why then should I not do what they say, which is to wait and see how the regulatory changes work out before going to a statutory solution?

Ms. SHAW. Madam Chair, I think one statement you made during the hearing a little earlier that sealed it for me was that if you stick to 5 days you will never know whether we really should have done 8 or should have done 10, that if you allow employees to use more and if they don't use them, well, fine, but if they need them, then what would be the point of denying it? And I think certainly, too, we would prefer to see this in statute as opposed to regulation.

Mr. HARNAGE. Yes, Madam Chairman, I think your observations were right on target, but the OPM's assumptions are flawed in that they simply are a matter of mathematics. They took 13 days and subtracted the average, the remainder was 5, and that is the reason they came up with the number of sick leave days that could be used.

Where that is flawed is, it is an average, and I think you are right in questioning their statistics where they come up with an explanation of how they reached that average. If it is the total number of 6 days used divided by the number of employees, then it is a very distorted average.

For example, if one employee who has bypass surgery is out 48 days, it would take five other employees using zero sick leave to get your average 8 days. My wife last year went through major neck surgery, and she was out 5½ months. It would have taken 20 other Federal employees taking zero sick leave in order to get your average.

This is the old concept of punishing the innocent and letting the guilty go free. We are telling an employee who has not used any sick leave, "Well, you are one of those average eight," whereas an other employee that may have used all 13, we are saying, "You are all right, on an average you only use eight."

But another problem I see with it is, it didn't take into consideration those individual leave balances. A person may have taken 6 months of sick leave because of major surgery or cancer or major illness but had that much accumulated sick leave they merely used each year as allowance and divided it by the total number of days used, which gives you a very distorted assumption, and I am glad to hear that you are going to pursue those statistics.

I was surprised at OPM's position, but I should not have been, having been in the business as long as I have, but going through the National Performance Review, the reinventing Government, where we are trying to make the Federal Government a better place to work, attract high caliber employees, and provide competitive benefits, and relieve some of the restrictions so that employees not only can decide their own welfare in life but how to do the Government job better and more efficiently, to not overmanage them any longer, and one of the things that I understood, part of the partnership concept and the reinventing Government was to lessen the role of OPM in micromanaging agencies and micromanaging Federal employees, but here they are taking a position of restricting what an agency can do with its employees without any really bona fide data to support that.

So all that is telling me is, old habits are hard to break. They still are playing the big brother role, and I think they have got to learn to get out of that.

Ms. NORTON. Well, you point up an important inconsistency between the flexibility of reinventing Government and the rigidity of at least part of their proposal, and we are going to hold them to the standard they have set for themselves.

I ask the ranking member if she has any further questions.

Mrs. MORELLA. No, except I guess you would agree that to have something that is the law is much more satisfying than having a regulation. And, finally, if any of you have any suggestions with regard to the legislation, is there anything that you would change if you had an opportunity to do so? Do you feel with this sunset provision, this is the way to go? I guess not.

I am also a long-distance care giver, so I can understand, again, not only the point of view from a sick child but the point of view, as you mentioned in our statistics, elderly parents, the needs that fall on our families now that were not there years ago because of medical science, because of two partners working, because of single heads of households.

Thank you. Thank you, Madam Chair.

Ms. NORTON. Thank you very much.

Thank you very much Ms. Morella, and I want to thank the four of you for very helpful testimony to the subcommittee.

The hearing is adjourned. Excuse me. Before I adjourn, just let me say the subcommittee has received statements from other employee organizations in support of this legislation, and I will see that that goes into the record and that the record remains open for 30 days for other organizations and individuals who may wish to submit testimony for or against the legislation.

The hearing is adjourned.

[Whereupon, at 3:46 p.m., the subcommittee was adjourned.]

[Additional material submitted for the record follows:]

PREPARED STATEMENT OF THE FEDERAL MANAGERS ASSOCIATION

Madam Chairwoman, members of the Subcommittee: FMA is the largest and oldest group of its kind, representing the interests of nearly 20,000 Federal managers and supervisors throughout the Federal government.

First, we would like to thank you for introducing the Federal Employees Family Friendly Leave Act, H.R. 4361, legislation to provide that Federal employees may use sick leave to attend to the needs of family members and to change the voluntary leave transfer program so that employees may transfer annual leave to family members. Second, we would like to thank you for inviting FMA to comment on this important legislation.

Since the release, last September, of the report of the National Performance Review [NPR], Creating a Government That Works Better and Costs Less, FMA, with your support, has been deeply involved in the reinvention process. Of all the people working for the Federal government, managers and supervisors are the most aware that our problems stem from the fact that we have good employees who are trapped in bad systems. With this in mind, FMA applauds and whole-heartedly supports your efforts to facilitate the implementation of provisions contained in NPR recommendation HRM07 "Enhancing Programs To Provide Family-Friendly Workplaces." The changes you propose in H.R. 4361 will truly make the government work better and cost less.

SICK LEAVE

The first session of the 103rd Congress saw the enactment of landmark legislation, the Family and Medical Leave Act of 1993 (P.L. 103–3). Under this law, as in the private sector Federal employees are entitled to 12 weeks of unpaid family and medical leave during a given 1 year period. Employees may take this unpaid leave for any of the following reasons: birth of a child, the placement of a son or daughter with the employee for adoption or foster care, the care of a spouse, son, daughter, or parent with a serious health condition, or a serious health condition which makes the employee unable to perform the essential functions of their job.

The ability to take leave to care for a sick child or close relative or to give birth represents a great step forward toward helping employees balance the needs of their family against the needs of their employers. Managers and supervisors know that employees are not productive and effective at work if they are needed at home to care for a sick child, spouse or parent.

On May 11, the Office of Personnel Management issued regulations to allow Federal employees to use up to five days of their own sick leave per year to care for their sick children, spouses, or parents or to arrange and attend the funeral services for those family members. FMA applauds this action to dramatically improve the ability of Federal workers to care for sick family members. Providing paid leave for this purpose will make it truly accessible to employees at all grade levels.

FMA supports the OPM's proposed regulation to extend paid sick leave for the purposes of arranging and/or attending the funeral of a child, spouse or parent. FMA sees this provision as a logical extension of the use of sick leave to care for a sick relative. In addition, FMA supports the provision in OPM's proposed regulations which would eliminate the current rule that Federal workers who have left service retain credit for their accumulated sick leave only if they return to work for the Federal Government within three years. With the current 5 year bar to reemployment for those accepting buyouts, this provision makes good sense. FMA urges the Subcommittee's favorable consideration for inclusion of both of these provisions in H.R. 4361.

ANNUAL LEAVE

Last year, the Compensation and Employee Benefits Subcommittee played a central role in enacting, the Federal Employees Leave Sharing Amendments Act of 1993 (P.L. 103–103). Under this law, the two leave programs established by the 1988 Federal Employees Leave Sharing Act (P.L. 100–566) are now permanent. Agencies are now allowed to offer both leave transfer and leave bank programs. Under the leave transfer program, Federal employees who have expended all their annual leave may accept donated leave from other employees during a personal or family medical emergency. Under the leave bank program, employees who are experiencing a personal or family medical emergency may accept leave which has been donated to a central leave bank. In addition, employees may participate in other agency's leave sharing programs.

OPM's report to Congress last year on the Federal Employees Leave Sharing Act indicated that leave sharing and leave bank programs produced savings for the government. Savings were realized because more leave was donated than was used and leave donors generally have higher salaries than leave recipients.

FMA supports the improvements to the leave sharing program proposed in H.R. 4361 to waive the current medical emergency requirement for Federal employees wishing to transfer annual leave to a family member.

FMA VIEWS ON SIMILAR LEGISLATION AND PROPOSALS

H.R. 2437

FMA would like to take this opportunity to express its support for legislation introduced by Post Office and Civil Service Committee member Representative Patricia Schroeder (D–CO), The Federal Family Education Leave Act, H.R. 2437. FMA has endorsed this legislation which would allow Federal employees to take up to 8 hours of unpaid leave a year to attend the education-related activities of their children. FMA urges favorable consideration of H.R. 2437.

Sick leave at military facilities slated for closure

FMA would also like to express support for introduction of legislation to allow Federal employees who are working at military bases which are scheduled to be closed to convert their unused sick leave toward satisfying retirement service and age requirements. Our members have found that employees at closing bases tend to use more sick leave. Allowing employees to convert their sick leave in the manner we propose would help closing bases perform their missions in a more efficient and productive manner. I would be happy to discuss this proposal in more detail with you or your staff.

PREPARED STATEMENT OF MARY CHATEL, PRESIDENT, NATIONAL COUNCIL, SOCIAL SECURITY MANAGEMENT ASSOCIATIONS, INC.

NATIONAL COUNCIL,
SOCIAL SECURITY MANAGEMENT ASSOCIATIONS, INC.,
West Warwick, RI, June 1, 1994.

Hon. ELEANOR HOLMES NORTON,
Chairwoman, Subcommittee on Compensation and Employee Benefits,
Washington, DC.

DEAR REPRESENTATIVE NORTON: Thank you for the invitation to appear before the Subcommittee earlier this month regarding H.R. 4361, the Family Friendly Leave Act. While we were unable to prepare a statement in advance of the hearing, our representative in Washington, Janet Garry, has spoken with your staff about our views. I understand that you are advancing the bill to mark-up right away, but if the record of the May 18 hearing is still open, please include this letter as our written statement.

First, our association deeply appreciates your many efforts to make the federal workplace both safe and flexible in the interest of federal employees. In Social Security field offices across the country, the managers and supervisors we represent know what it takes to make a good team effort to serve the public. Like you, we believe that productivity and quality of service are enhanced when employees are treated with respect and flexibility.

We therefore support the intent of both parts of H.R. 4361—to allow sick leave to be used to care for a family member who is ill and to allow transfers of annual leave among federal employees in the same family for non-medical reasons. We all know of situations where these authorities would have well served the needs of ourselves and our staffs in making arrangements to balance work responsibilities with pressing family demands and difficulties.

We are extremely sympathetic to the need to help responsible, hardworking employees who must deal with the stresses of juggling competing demands. We suggest, however, an approach which either: (1) limits the use of accumulated sick leave to family situations in which there is a family health care emergency or severe illness; or (2) limits the number of days of sick leave which can be used for family care, such as OPM has proposed in setting a restriction of five days per year.

The reason for our cautious approach is that, as managers and supervisors, we deal every day with workplace problems caused by abuses of the leave system. As a result of extensive FTE reductions at SSA—downsizing which is now being replicated in many federal agencies—it is more important than ever that we have sufficient employees at work each day to handle our workloads. When employees are out, it impacts all the others on our hardworking teams in SS field offices as well as affecting the public we serve. As managers, we assume responsibility for managing normal absenteeism on a day-to-day basis. Sometimes this is a formidable challenge, especially in our smaller offices or when employees are out for extended periods. While GAO reports that 36 percent of "leading employers" in the private sector have liberalized leave policies, how many small businesses, to which our field offices are more comparable, can do the same and maintain full operations? We are concerned that further liberalization of federal employee leave policies may compound the problems, especially those created when employees are out for extended periods.

We believe that responsible employees, knowing that the government has no short-term disability program, should try to accumulate sick leave for their own future use. Some employees, however, do not use their sick leave wisely, and they may have an even greater problem—or have it sooner—when they need their leave unexpectedly if current policies are liberalized to the degree you recommend. Anecdotal evidence suggests, for example, that many employees who apply for leave transfers under current law are those who did not accumulate their own sick leave all along. Candidly, it creates a dilemma for fellow employees who must consider whether to give annual leave to a co-worker who needs it for medical reasons, if the co-workers' need is perceived to have developed as a result of abuse of sick leave policies.

These aspects of leave programs may be at risk of being overlooked because they are unpleasant to think about. We all want to assume the best of one another rather than try to evaluate how widespread abuse might become. As hands-on managers and supervisors accountable for the operations of over 1,300 field offices each day, however, we must necessarily take a reality-based view. We believe that liberalization of annual leave transfers and sick leave policies should proceed in a measured way so that federal agencies can evaluate the impact of Congress can then make an all-things-considered decision about whether to further modify our leave policies.

Thank you for considering our views.

Sincerely,

MARY CHATEL, *President.*

○

9780160461989